Central St.Martins College of Art and Design Library

University of the Arts London
Central
Saint Martins

URBAN COMPOSITION

Developing Community through Design

Mark C. Childs

PRINCETON ARCHITECTURAL PRESS · NEW YORK

DEDICATED TO
Elaine, Emily, and Quinault. Now it's your turn to
write a book.

ACKNOWLEDGMENTS
I deeply appreciate the gracious assistance of
Elaine Thomas, Dorothy Thomas, Mazohra Glynn-Thami,
Judith Wong, Doug Eberhart, and Megan Carey, as well
as my students, editors, and reviewers, and the
contributors of photographs.

Portions of this work are based on previously published
articles by the author, including:
"A Spectrum of Urban Design Roles," *Journal of Urban
   Design* 15, no. 1 (2010): 1–19.
"Civic Concinnity," *Journal of Urban Design* 14, no. 2
   (2009): 131–45.
"Storytelling and Urban Design," *Journal of Urbanism* 1,
   no. 2 (2008): 173–86.
"Civic Ecosystems," *Journal of Urban Design* 6, no. 1
   (2001): 52–72.

PUBLISHED BY
Princeton Architectural Press
37 East 7th Street
New York, NY 10003

For a free catalog of books, call 1-800-722-6657
Visit our website at www.papress.com

© 2012 Princeton Architectural Press
All rights reserved
Printed and bound in China
15 14 13 12 4 3 2 1 First edition

COVER IMAGE: Gary718 Stock Photography

EDITOR: Megan Carey
DESIGNER: Paul Wagner

SPECIAL THANKS TO
Bree Anne Apperley, Sara Bader, Nicholas Beatty,
Nicola Bednarek Brower, Janet Behning, Fannie Bushin,
Carina Cha, Russell Fernandez, Jan Haux, Linda Lee,
Diane Levinson, Jennifer Lippert, Gina Morrow,
John Myers, Katharine Myers, Margaret Rogalski,
Elana Schlenker, Dan Simon, Sara Stemen,
Andrew Stepanian, and Joseph Weston of
Princeton Architectural Press —Kevin C. Lippert, publisher

LIBRARY OF CONGRESS
CATALOGING-IN-PUBLICATION DATA
Childs, Mark C.
Urban composition : developing community through
design / Mark C. Childs. — 1st ed.
     p. cm. — (Architecture briefs series)
Includes bibliographical references.
ISBN 978-1-61689-052-0 (alk. paper)
   1. City planning—Social aspects. 2. Architecture—
Human factors. I. Title. II. Title: Developing community
through design.
NA9053.H76C49 2012
711'.4—dc23
                                        2011043094

The Architecture Briefs series takes on a variety of single topics of interest to architecture students and young professionals. Field-specific and technical information are presented in a user-friendly manner along with basic principles of design and construction. The series familiarizes readers with the concepts and technical terms necessary to successfully translate ideas into built form.

ALSO IN THIS SERIES

Architects Draw
Sue Ferguson Gussow
ISBN 978-1-56898-740-8

Architectural Lighting:
Designing with Light and Space
Hervé Descottes, Cecilia E. Ramos
ISBN 978-1-56898-938-9

Architectural Photography
the Digital Way
Gerry Kopelow
ISBN 978-1-56898-697-5

Building Envelopes:
An Integrated Approach
Jenny Lovell
ISBN 978-1-56898-818-4

Digital Fabrications:
Architectural and Material
Techniques
Lisa Iwamoto
ISBN 978-1-56898-790-3

Ethics for Architects:
50 Dilemmas of Professional Practice
Thomas Fisher
ISBN 978-1-56898-946-4

Material Strategies:
Innovative Applications in Architecture
Blaine Brownell
ISBN 978-1-56898-986-0

Model Making
Megan Werner
ISBN 978-1-56898-870-2

Old Buildings, New Designs:
Architectural Transformations
Charles Bloszies
ISBN 978-1-61689-035-3

Philosophy for Architects
Branko Mitrović
ISBN 978-1-56898-994-5

Sustainable Design:
A Critical Guide
David Bergman
ISBN 978-1-56898-941-9

Writing about Architecture:
Mastering the Language of Buildings
and Cities
Alexandra Lange
ISBN 978-1-61689-053-7

Introduction

Introduction

> The basic idea of city planning is the clear recognition of the fact that no one can accept responsibility for any smallest element in the complex unit that we call a city without participating also in the joint, undivided, and complex responsibility for the future excellence or inferiority of the city as a whole.
> —FREDERICK LAW OLMSTED, *American City Magazine*, 1913

How can civil designers—architects, landscape architects, civil engineers, public artists, city council members, and others—collaborate in the collective work of creating environmentally sound, socially resilient, and soul-enlivening settlements?

Settlements are among our greatest creations, yet no single individual or organization creates them. The gardens, buildings, streets, power substations, public artworks, and other built forms of even a small town embody substantial investments of money, natural resources, social capital, and dreams. But settlements are not just the sums of their parts; their poetry and vitality comes from their *collective* composition—the interactions among multiple designs. Sometimes the places that emerge are glorious. Too frequently they are not.

Panorama of Rome showing the city's evolved urban fabric, from *Baedeker's Central Italy*, 1897.

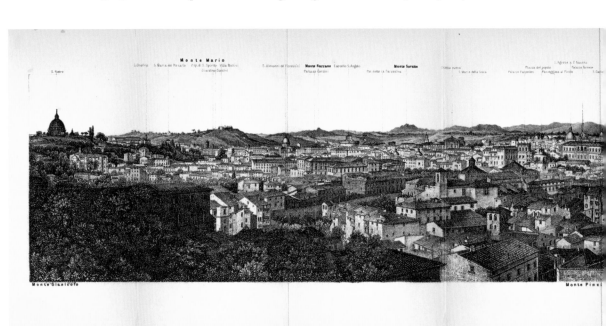

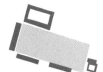

ca. 1609

ca. 1660

ca. 1694

right
Approximate diagrams of the
evolution of the plaza in Santa Fe,
New Mexico, redrawn from aerials,
Sanborn maps, the 1846 Gilmer
map, the 1766 Urrutia map, and
written records of the Spanish
foundation and reconquest.
Diagrams before 1766 are highly
speculative. The two kivas, partially
underground structures used by
Pueblo Indians for religious
purposes, and other features are
mentioned in written reports.

1766

1846

1883

2008

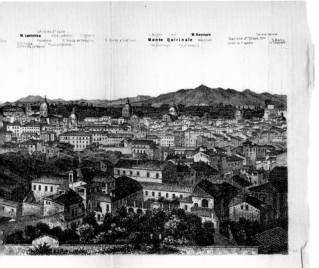

PANORAMA DI ROMA
preso da S.Pietro

This primer is an introduction to urban composition for designers, community members, and other stakeholders of individual projects. It aims to help you creatively contribute to the environmentally sound, socially robust, and inspiring composition of vibrant settlements.

To play improvisational jazz, it is necessary not only to master an instrument but also to collaborate and feel the direction and possibilities of the music. To tend an ecosystem, one must understand not only individual species, but also the complex interactions of species over time and place. Similarly, to help compose settlements, one must be able not only to design a building, landscape, public work, or other built form, but also to contribute to their emergent collective character.[1] This mastery requires, at minimum, a robust understanding of a project's potential contexts (see "Contexts"), the roles that types of built forms play within their contexts (see "Built Species"), approaches to defining which contexts are critical (see "Framing and Reframing"), ways to inspire others and add to the composition (see "Infectious Design"), and knowledge of how to work with "design editors" who are the stewards of settlements (see "Design Editors"). The order of these chapters is not meant to imply a step-by-step design process, but rather to provide a conceptual framework.

These chapters rest on an understanding of three concepts: "civil settlements," "civil composition," and a spectrum of "civil design roles," as outlined below.

Civil Settlements

Because the ways we live together on the planet have changed, it is difficult to choose the correct words to describe our collective compositions of built forms. *Urban* suggests a density of interacting buildings, but in common usage that term discounts towns, villages, and cultural landscapes. *Civic* suggests a collective goal but means "relating to municipal government" and thus excludes nongovernmental collective composition. I propose *civil*—meaning relating to citizenship, public life, and civilization—to imply an ecosystem of independent designers making interacting design decisions that contribute to our shared environment.

Because, at least in the United States, both professional practice and academia use the term *urban* to speak about a congregation of built forms, I will use both *civil composition* and *urban composition* throughout the book with the understanding that *urban* includes a range of settlements.

Following the Latin roots *civitas* and *urbanitas*, I will use *civil* to stress collective goals and *urban* to emphasize built forms.

Civil settlements emerge from multiple independent projects. Company towns and many resort villages, designed and administered by a single corporation, are not civil settlements but rather large works of architecture and landscape architecture. They may become densely woven settlements as additions, modifications, and other changes accumulate. Wilderness areas, except in the design of their boundaries and trails, are uncomposed by humans. On the other hand, a village with a few independently created buildings forming a square or commons may be a small but poetic civil settlement.

Settlements range in scale from hamlets to continent-spanning forms. We have created whistle-stops, the medina of Marrakesh, edge cities, Devonshire's weave of farm and village, Holland's polders, Roman and Incan road networks, the charm bracelet of Alaskan cruise-ship towns, the Taiheiyō Belt (Ibaraki Prefecture to Fukuoka Prefecture in Japan), the U.S. land ordinance survey grid, and the filament of development along the trans-Siberian railway.

Urban settlements arise within and from amalgamations of landforms, economics, building traditions, and other contexts, and often have a palette of characteristic built-form types, such as the canals and canal houses of Amsterdam. However, customs and innovations of building are increasingly shared between civil settlements. Following the economic and cultural success of Frank Gehry's 1997 Guggenheim Museum in Bilbao, Spain, the "Bilbao effect"—branding cities with emblematic museums—has influenced communities

The world at night. This image shows large cultural landscape patterns such as the trans-Siberian filaments, the U.S. interstate system, and the preference for seaside property.

Trampas, a typical settlement of colonial northern New Mexico. The town is composed of a plaza and church, farm homes and barns, and acequias (irrigation canals) and croplands, set within a watered valley, crossed by the high road to Taos in the juniper-piñon hills below Trampas Peak. Shown below are a bell tower on a general store, a hay barn, irrigated fields in the valley bottom, and an acequia crossing a valley.

and designers across the world. Variations of many built-form patterns, such as bungalows, boulevards, and even ATM vestibules, are found around the globe. Dutch development of residential streets shared between drivers and pedestrians is cited as a precedent by urban design students in New Mexico. Designers and design firms cross borders, bringing concepts and approaches with them.

Cosmopolitan culture, in many parts of the world, is no longer a monopoly of the metropolis. Settlements of all sizes may be urbane. Art dealers and stockbrokers work from once-remote Andean mountain slopes. The World Economic Forum meets in the small Swiss town of Davos. Art communities, university towns, and other "cultural capital" settlements actively seek to be cosmopolitan.[2] Mass migration has provided even remote places with multiple cuisines, spatial practices, and customs of building. Access to the world's cornucopia of music, literature, photography, architectural monographs, film, and other forms of culture is limited largely by bandwidth, not proximity. This global cosmopolitanism, while offering benefits, can run roughshod over local culture, outshout community stories, and denigrate local tastes.

The development of nested urban compositions up to the size of continents, distributed cosmopolitan culture, and the potential worldwide dialogue of built forms all imply a global urbanity. In important senses, the world has taken on characteristics of the classic city. The taxonomy of city, town, village, countryside, etcetera, remains valuable for description but should no longer imply a spectrum from city sophisticate to village rube.

Prada Marfa installation by Michael Elmgreen and Ingar Dragset, twenty-six miles outside of Marfa, Texas, 2005. This artwork plays on the modern complexity of cosmopolitanism.

Yet settlements can be more or less profoundly composed, depending on the diversity, elaboration, density, eloquence, and import of the relationships between the built parts. Too many of our landscapes are poorly composed: Their built forms don't add up to much more than an adjacency of parts. For example, interstate villages—those aggregations of motels, gas stations, and fast-food outlets around freeway exits—could be substantially more sustainable, convivial, and poetic. They pale in comparison to their kin from earlier eras, such as the European crossroads inn, tavern, and stables, or the Silk Road caravansaries.

There are many different types and characteristics of remarkable urban settlements. Istanbul is profoundly different from Taos Pueblo, and both differ from the wine region of Napa, California, and the territory of southwestern French *bastides*. Richly composed settlements interweave built claims and counterclaims responding to the fabric of contexts (see "Contexts") in which confluences of goals and form—built-form species—have meaning (see "Built Species").

below, left
Büyük Han in Nicosia, Cyprus. This sixteenth-century caravansary was an inn, stable, and market.

right
Sidewalk, Cuernavaca, Mexico. In a design that reframes the existing conditions, a sidewalk along a blank wall has been transformed into a canyon garden.

Civil Composition

The Latin term *concinnus* means "deftly joined." Our descendent term, *concinnity*, means the skillful and harmonious adaptation or fitting together of parts to craft a whole. Civil composition relies on a concinnity in which multiple independently designed parts collectively make vibrant streets, districts, towns, and other settlements. As the design critic Paul Goldberger writes:

> This is the single most important principle of urban architecture: the whole is more than the sum of its parts. That doesn't mean that the parts need to be the same or that they need to be subjugated to the whole.... But it does mean that for a city to work, architects need to feel as if they are designing a section of a much larger composition, a composition that began long before them and will continue long after them.[3]

Great places emerge from the concinnity of incremental acts of design. Existing work frames new projects, which in turn inspire future works (see "Framing and Reframing" and "Infectious Design").

A lack of concinnity can be seen in identical franchise stores, manufactured housing units, and much infrastructure design. Ignoring many of their contexts, they fail to create larger forms, such as a small-town main street. Without these larger forms, individual projects stand or die on their own. They don't benefit from district synergies, such as the

Main street, Telluride, Colorado. "Poetry," Octavio Paz writes in *The Other Voice*, "is governed by the twofold principle of 'variety within unity.'" The delight of a classic main street comes from its variety of building styles, sizes, and uses within a set of ordering conventions that help enclose and activate it.

mutually beneficial relationships between theaters and restaurants. Excessive independence causes inefficiencies, such as duplicate parking, disconnected sidewalks, and poorly defined streets. Moreover, even a single built place that ignores its context can erode collective forms. For example, in the midst of a sidewalk shopping district, a retail chain store with a streetside parking lot can weaken the district. Users' adaptations, fortuitous juxtapositions, and well-conceived new projects may subsequently weave these built forms into a rich composition, but such actions are repairs to the fabric and do not justify the original designers' lack of engagement.

Civil composition, however, is not just any concinnity of parts. It aims to produce environments that enable and support not only private goals but also the commonwealth. The goals of the commonwealth are a matter of public debate and wisdom. However, in the interests of engaging the debate and making clear the principles underlying this book, I suggest seven intertwined public goals for civil composition (see sidebar on page 19).

Sustainable, convivial, healthy, and soul-enlivening places require a well-tempered concinnity. Our towns and landscapes too frequently suffer from a lack of concinnity, overbearing concinnity (where order is unduly dictated), or superficial concinnity, in which a built form responds to its contexts in a manner that does not add to the commonwealth but rather trivializes or denigrates collective composition.[4]

Overbearing concinnity frequently occurs when what should be multiple independent projects are aggregated into a single development. Like a monoculture forest plantation, this "single-hand" composition often engenders a set of problems. Monotony of repetition replaces the vibrancy and resilience of multiple designs. Critiques of chain stores, tract housing, freeways, telephone lines, and industrial farming all point to this problem.[5] Like aggregation of the news media, large developments often fail to nurture a creative and democratic forum. They allow few venues for designs that are new, unfamiliar, or unproven in the marketplace, or designs that are farsighted, dissenting, or in the minority. Such developments can contribute to creating a political or economic hegemony. Finally, in overplayed concinnity, urban form becomes a "product" for what the sociologist and philosopher Jürgen Habermas calls a culture-consuming society, rather than the result of a culture-debating society.[6] Stage-set-like compositions are created for consumers and staffed by "cast members." Main Street in Disneyland has a variety of buildings, a street,

Civil Composition for the Collective Good

Relationships between built forms and social practices are complex and recursive.
Physical design cannot invent a creative milieu from scratch or ensure environmental
stewardship. People may, for example, overheat a building designed to be environmentally
efficient. Well-designed sidewalks may enable and encourage people to walk rather
than drive, but there's no guarantee that they will, and a society that already values walking
is more likely to invest in sidewalks.

     Yet, with clear goals, built forms can add to the vitality of a settlement. They have
the power to dispirit or inspire, deter or encourage, show disregard or social investment.
I propose the following goals not as the definitive goals of good civil composition but
rather as provisional guides to framing the welter of potential contexts and judging the
quality of composition:

1 — **Stewardship** of our biotic contexts and built heritage. Reducing our carbon footprint
and conserving historic buildings are parts of this stewardship.

2 — **Promoting public health and safety**, including traditional concerns, such as disease
and fire suppression, as well as more recently articulated goals, such as enabling walking
and healthy lifestyles.

3 — **Providing economic foundations**, including collective infrastructure. Public bridges
and farmers' markets, for example, provide economic opportunity.

4 — **Building a vital public realm** that supports and represents conviviality and civil
society. Buildings can enliven the streets or plazas they face, for example.

5 — **Enabling creative milieus** for the pursuit of happiness, creativity, and wisdom.[7] The
renowned urbanist Peter Hall argues that dense pedestrian districts have been centers
of creative efflorescence.[8]

6 — **Elaboration of a poetically rich genius loci**. Great places are poetically rich. One's
attachment to their home landscape arises from their personal stories of place embedded in
the cultural spirit of place, the genius loci. The sense of the numinous or poetic has been a
central concern of designers across cultures and eras. A web of interrelated, deeply
considered built forms, elaborations, counterclaims, avant-garde revolutions, and revivals
gives rise to the emergent character of profound places, such as the Tuscan landscape,
Jerusalem, Varanasi and the Ganges, or Oxford. Strong civil composition pursues all the
criteria above; inspired composition does so in a way that adds resonance
to the genius loci.

7 — **Open systems** that allow for variety, reinterpretation, and dissent. The British
professor John Niles says of great oral poems such as *Beowulf* that they are "a collective,
even restive, engagement with the question of what wisdom is."[9] The design decisions
of civil composition should embody an open struggle with the same question.

and a square, but it is a single design made for entertainment, which copies the surface forms of an emergent place but not the generative principles. As a playground it can be delightful, but it is not a model for urban composition. Over time a development that was over-controlled may be modified by subsequent owners and create a more balanced concinnity. Current-day Levittown, New York, for example, has been rebuilt and enriched by multiple generations of homeowners.[10] Superficial or mock concinnity is akin to bad poetry. It neither provides utility nor evokes profound meaning. Narrow definitions of context miss the productive struggle with the complexities, multiple histories, and nuances of place. Like adding plastic flowers to a forest meadow, mock concinnity at best has a touch of wit but ultimately fails to engage the ecosystem. It is a play of technique over content.

A feel for the ongoing enterprise of civil composition, balancing between the poverty of a lack of concinnity, overbearing order, and trivial harmony, is essential for creating great places.

Spectrum of Roles: Civil Designers and Editors

In many professions there are people who address individual cases and others who address systemwide and public issues. In medicine, for example, general-practice doctors take care of individuals, and public health officials focus on the general population. Authors write texts; editors commission and compose those texts into magazines and books. Frequently, practitioners of case and systemic work come from the same set of disciplines: Judges are typically lawyers, public health officers are often nurses and doctors, and editors frequently come from the ranks of writers. In civil composition, "civil designers"—the designers of parks, streets, buildings, and other built forms—focus on individual cases; "civil editors"—design reviewers, subdivision designers and developers, pattern

below, left

Daly City, California. In 1962 Malvina Reynolds wrote the song "Little Boxes" to lampoon the Westlake neighborhood of Daly City and similar developments composed of nearly identical houses with poor construction ("ticky-tacky") and only superficial variation ("There's a green one and a pink one") within a milieu of bourgeois conformity ("And they all play on the golf course / And drink their martinis dry"). This critique is valid for many postwar suburban developments.

below, right

Warehouse adorned with faux silhouettes of houses, Albuquerque. The warehouse mocks the idea of responding to context. There may be ironic wit in the gesture, but it fails to offer anything of substance.

book writers, etcetera—commission, review, and orchestrate systems for good compositions and settlements.

Civil designers and editors have obligations to provide both private and collective goods. Just as private doctors have responsibilities to their individual patients and the health of the wider public, designers of single buildings, parking lots, and power lines are also responsible for how they help shape larger settlements. This encompasses more than complying with the letter of regulations. The nuances and particular conditions of these collective goods are often beyond the reasonable reach of regulation and must be addressed by the designer's judgment.

Because of the different roles that civil designers and editors play, there is a creative tension: Designers pull toward the particular and editors toward the systemic. This tension of variety within order, order arising from variety, or a variety of collaged orders is the essence of civil composition. Neither designer nor editor should dominate, yet both should advocate their respective position (see "Design Editors").

Civil composition that aims to enrich the common-wealth is a more democratic, adaptable, diverse, and resilient approach to creating vibrant settlements than either large-scale, single-hand design or each-for-their-own, noncontextual design. It does not promise instant planet-changing revolution or unconstrained individual expression, but rather the action-by-action evolution of a vital community.

Skyscrapers along the Chicago River. The emergence of this skyscraper district can be viewed as a cycle of boasting in which each work provided the inspiration and basis for comparison for later ones, but together they created a distinct place and incited other cities to follow.

Contexts

Contexts

The history of a venerable old city is like a ledger account for the tremendous sums of spiritual, mental, and artistic capital that have been invested in it.
—CAMILLO SITTE

What is context? How can a project's designers respond to its contexts in ways that enrich the immediate project, future remodels, and other forms it helps compose?

Descending from the Latin term for "weaving together," the word *context* refers to the circumstances that surround a thing or an event. Urban context is the set of conditions that frame a project's potential meaning and that, in turn, the project can redefine. A statue at the terminus of a street is both understood in the context of the street and restructures the meaning of the street. Context is complex and open to reinterpretation, and defining the critical contexts is a fundamental act of design.

Context should be differentiated from site. The site is the physical location of a project that is under the designer's direct control. Context includes the site and larger physical and conceptual landscapes in which the project takes place. This distinction separates the area of control from the area of influence, and reminds designers that there are important considerations outside of their immediate jurisdiction. A grocery store, for example, can help extend a window-shopping street or erode it, depending on how it engages the sidewalk. It can also affect neighborhood traffic, modify adjacent stream flows, or set a design precedent by incorporating a stage for parking lot concerts or space for a demonstration garden.

Too often, context analysis consists solely of examining engineering aspects of the property. Such a site analysis typically includes topography and hydrology, solar exposure, utility location, nuisances such as noise, and adjacent automobile traffic counts. It misses the built history of the milieu, the stories of place, the program of the surrounding location, and many other aspects of context.

Thinking of context as "local surroundings" too often limits inquiry. Is it only the buildings next door that provide context? We may think of *local* as implying the immediate vicinity. However, the first definition of *local* in the *Oxford English Dictionary* begins, "pertaining to or concerned with place." In this more expansive view, the scale that *local* refers to depends on the issue at hand. Humankind is local to the Earth.

This parking garage in San Diego clearly has effects beyond its site. Perhaps it would be a better neighbor if the house-side wall was a heavily planted green wall.

The *local school*, however, does not mean any school on the planet. If we are concerned about water quality, the watershed is the local context, but for greenhouse gases, the planet's atmosphere is the appropriate context.

Design projects sit within myriad contexts at multiple scales. A creek restoration project, for example, may need to take into account the sewer systems and water-harvesting possibilities of buildings within the watershed, spawning habits of fish, law-enforcement concerns, street design standards, children's play habits, and climate change. Civil designers should examine a rich range of contexts.

Each combination of program, ecosystem, built context, narrative landscape, design participants, and other contexts produces a unique field of design possibilities. This chapter discusses types of contexts that shape projects and should normally be part of context analysis.

The parking garage on this New Orleans street was carefully designed to blend with the existing context.

The Land

▶   In what ways might a project be conditioned
     by, and in turn nurture, the ecological environment?

In *Nature's Metropolis: Chicago and the Great West*, the environmental historian William Cronon richly details how Chicago's rise rested on development of millions of square miles of ecological, cultural, and economic frontier.[1] Ecosystems are vital contexts. We must be attuned to the roles our projects play in the carbon cycle, watersheds, epidemiologic pathways, and more. Two of the twenty-first century's most important challenges are rebalancing the amount of carbon in the atmosphere and building settlements that are resilient to climate changes. Three overlapping aspects of environmental context are sustainability, stewardship, and genius loci.

Sustainability

Many definitions of *sustainability* point to the intertwined goals of natural, social, and economic vitality, and suggest that sustainability means long-term maintenance of the vitality of the biosphere in a manner that supports humankind's well-being. Sustainability, at a minimum, requires that we be judicious in our use of environmental resources and that we build places that can adapt to environmental and social flux.

Drawing of a dovecote designed by Coolidge & Carlson, from *The Country House* by C. E. Cooper, 1905. Studying old agricultural structures, sites, and patterns may aid rediscovery of approaches to environmental fit.

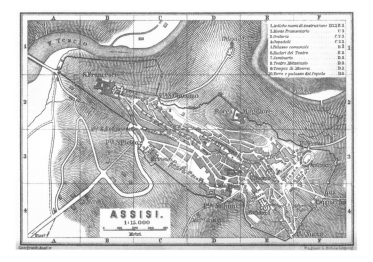

Map of Assisi, Italy, showing the town along the ridge of a hill, commanding bends in the river, from *Baedeker's Central Italy*, 1897.

To skillfully situate a built form, patterns of sunlight, soil, water, and wind around a site must be studied. Techniques of daylight and water harvesting, ventilation, shade making, shielding from winds, earth coupling (using the temperature of the ground to moderate a building's temperature), evapotranspiration (evaporation and plant transpiration), and other means of microclimate shaping and resource harvesting should be well-developed skills for civil designers. All of these skills, of course, require nuanced readings of the climate and the land.

Beyond harvesting the environmental resources that a context offers, we are responsible for our designs' demands on the ecological environment—what the ecologists and planners Mathis Wackernagel and William E. Rees call a project's "ecological footprint."[2] Where and how do we cut wood for lumber, mine stone, make plastics? How do leftovers from construction and maintenance become raw materials rather than wastes? What are the upstream sources and downstream deposits of our materials and fuels? We cannot responsibly build cities without also being accountable for the regional landscapes that support them.

In addition to harvesting site resources and shaping off-site effects, sustainability suggests designing for resiliency. By mapping the extents of a two-hundred-year flood, a two-meter sea level rise, an adjacent forest fire, a northward shift of habitats, and other potential changes, people can create designs that adapt to, or avoid, these possibilities.

Brickpit Ring Walk by Durbach Block Architects and Sue Barnsley Design, Sydney Olympic Park, Australia, 2005. A circular viewing platform hovers above a quarry that supplied most of the red brick used in Sydney's houses from 1910 to 1988. After the quarry's closure, it became a habitat for endangered Green and Golden Bell frogs, precluding many uses of the site for the Sydney Olympics. This interpretive center reframes the Brickpit as a sublime work of postindustrial land art.

The concept of ecological footprint, the landscape needed to build and operate a project, should be elaborated to describe the multifaceted interactions between natural and built landscapes. For example, many species use our objects and architecture as their habitats. The snails on this shoe insert on Miami Beach, the frogs in the Brickpit quarry, peregrine falcons on the ledges of skyscrapers, and others live in our built landscapes. Designers should aim to support appropriate and rich ecological use.

Stewardship

The extinction of the dodo did not imperil our survival, but it was an iniquitous act that diminished us. Our relationship with ecosystems is complex. Our built forms become habitats for other species. Telephone poles look like tree snags to many birds, and stormwater storage ponds can become intermittent wetlands. Our responsibility is not simply to manage how well the environment can support us, but to steward the diversity, resilience, and vitality of the world's life. Robust context analysis includes examining designs from the point of view of the species whose habitat they affect. Doing so can reveal possibilities to improve habitats, such as planting butterfly migration corridors. It can also illuminate problems to avoid, such as creating an ideal skunk habitat under a porch.

Genius Loci

Many cultures have venerated the numinous presence of places. We borrow the Latin term *genius loci* to talk about the phenomenological presence of a place. The British poet and garden designer Alexander Pope was an early proponent of this concept. In his 1731 *An Epistle to Burlington*, he declared that in architecture and gardening, "All must be adapted to the genius of the place, and...beauties not forced into it, but resulting from it."[3] The spirit of place, the genius loci, is formed by the folds of the land, the moods of the sky, the mosaic of flora and fauna, the stories of place, and the traditions of cultivation and building. The American landscape architect Horace Cleveland argued for designing with the genius loci in mind in his 1873 publication *Landscape Architecture, as Applied to the Wants of the West*. He suggested that new towns should be carefully sited in existing terrain and critical features retained as a surrounding open-space network.[4] These design considerations would add value to settlements that would not be gained from an uncontextualized real estate plan. A century later, the Norwegian architect Christian Norberg-Schulz described three phenomenological ways of being in the world, three broad categories of genius loci: romantic (northern forests), cosmic (desert places), and classical.[5]

Humans love the land, and studies have shown various benefits from access to nearby nature. For example, hospital patients heal faster with less pain medication if they have visual access to flora.[6] Playing with the environment—flying kites, enjoying fountains, gardening—is a central joy of humankind, which is reflected in our great places.

Moreover, there is a deep history in poetry, religion, music, and many other fields that attests to the importance of genius loci. A good part of who we are is the places we have lived. We are shaped by frozen forests under moonlight, the evening warmth of rock walls in the desert, the immensity of a prairie sky.

▶▶   *Study the land to build sustainably, be a good steward of the environment, and engage the poetry of the landscape. Diagram the spatial structure of the landform. Learn the habits and haunts of the flora and fauna. Eat local specialties. Listen to local language. Think like a painter and capture the sky. Camp on the land to experience its different moods. Build drafts of windows, walls, or gardens with temporary materials on the site.*

St. Michael's Mount, United Kingdom. At low tide the island is accessible by a causeway. This integration of the built environment with the landscape engenders a rich sense of story, a strong genius loci.

Built Venues and Precedents

▶   What are appropriate sets of projects against which to judge your work?

Ålesund, Norway. The built fabric of multistory Jugendstil buildings, waterfront and inland streets, and forested greens establishes a venue of precedents and relationships by which new projects will be judged.

Like players of a Scrabble game, designers create a significant portion of one another's context. Rather than being adversaries, however, the goal is the joint creation of vital settlements.

Collections of built forms are the result of designers' attempts at wrestling with overlapping sets of contexts and creating gracious coherence. There are two types of these collections: built venues and the canon of precedents.

Built Venues

A built venue is the field of built forms in which a project takes place—the district, town, or region. The coherence of these built forms is another ingredient in the genius loci. Projects take physical form here: sitting in the shadow of neighboring buildings, hosting uninvited pigeons, lining a street. Built venues are not just the surrounding built forms but may range from the neighborhood to the town, region, or larger cultural landscape.

Built venues emerge from the interactions of a whole culture, including designers and builders, mayors and councils, poets and bankers. The venues typically develop a set of conventional project types, such as Philadelphia brownstones, cricket fields, or Pueblan kivas; shared public spaces, such as a main street or the town square; design domains, such as plats within a block and street pattern; systems of design, such as Euclidian zoning, tract housing, or feng shui; and stories of place. These patterns of built form are an accumulation of cultural capital, honed convention, and knowledge about a way of life.

New Children's Museum by Rob Wellington Quigley, San Diego, 2008. The bays of the museum echo the size of earlier plats and thus buildings in the district, establishing a scale that both fits with existing patterns and creates more comfortable rooms and facades than would a building based on a whole-block scale.

Designers should not only study these venues, but also judge their work against their standards. Too frequently, designers have treated venues as restrictive molds to be dramatically broken, and thus have dismissed the long-term investments of a community. A venue's practices are not undue limits on creativity. Rather, they allow many different designs to develop independently within the social-political-economic coherence of a venue.

Built venues and their conventions are often remarkably long-lived. The Cairo bazaar district has existed for more than a thousand years and shows kinship with the

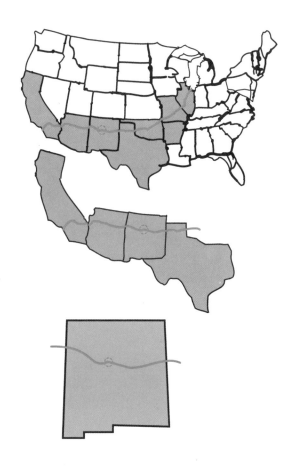

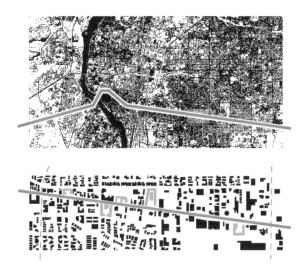

These maps show the scale of built venues for Route 66 motels (shown in blue in the bottom diagram) in the Nob Hill district of Albuquerque. The socioeconomic context of Route 66, the cultural narratives of the Southwest, the styles and references of New Mexico, the real estate market of Albuquerque, and the business milieu of Nob Hill are all contexts in which these motels were created and evolved.

2000 BCE field of Ur.[7] The landscape and collective institutions of *huertas*, ditch-irrigated farmlands around small villages in southeastern Spain, have thrived for 550 to one thousand years.[8] They are habitats for ways of life that have proved durable and should be respected and researched.

Precedents

Professional precedents are typically individual projects documented as case studies. Frequently, they form canons of "great works," which influence professional aspirations. A robust knowledge of the canons can inform new designs and allow participation in a built dialogue about great urban design.

Clock tower of King Street Station in Seattle, designed by Reed and Stem Architects, 1904. This tower is directly inspired by the campanile in Piazza San Marco, Venice, and is arguably too close a copy.

Professional precedents are typically not physically present in the vicinity of a project, and thus citizens, users, and designers may not have firsthand experience with them. Study of precedents is typically secondary research, and one can only evaluate what is documented. On the other hand, studying a built venue generally requires primary research: collecting data from the field in your own areas of interest, such as where people congregate or how a material weathers in the local climate. Both the strengths and the weaknesses of projects within the venue are accessible. When comparing precedent studies against primary research in a built venue, one must understand that precedents are often selected and presented as prime examples and often do not show weaknesses. However, as case studies, they frequently come with commentary and are situated within a body of theory.

Not all precedents are applicable to a particular project. Useful precedents illuminate some aspects of a project's critical contexts and provide substantive ideas for responding to them. For instance, the architect Renzo Piano's Jean-Marie Tjibaou Cultural Center (1998) in New Caledonia provides a strong example of drawing upon a local building culture while competing in the global context of iconic cultural centers.

Jean-Marie Tjibaou Cultural Center by Renzo Piano, New Caledonia, 1998

This precedent could help a designer contemplate the character of an airport intended to represent the region in a national network, but it may not be pertinent to a private home. Likewise, San Francisco's Embarcadero and Boston's Big Dig provide alternatives for Seattle as it considers options for its waterfront freeway.

Precedents may not come from professional "great works" or the latest design stars. "Cracker houses," tree-lined residential "Elm Streets," or "surfer shacks" may inspire owners and designers, for example.[9] Historic districts enforce the patterns of the district as precedents for new construction, and restrictive covenants often include design codes referencing an established style. The choice of precedents proclaims an alliance with a cultural mode.

Designers sometimes take sides by advocating solely for the vernacular built venue or for the development of a professional canon. As in many disputes, it is essential to ask why is this an either/or issue and who stands to gain from the quarrel. Design commissions almost always have embedded conflicts. They are exercises of power, and one design for a site precludes countless others. Yet blind allegiance to one context over another rules out common ground, possible synergies, and a creative tension that may yield new approaches. Just as the Supreme Court seeks to provide justice for the case at hand *and* coherently develop the law, civil designers can enrich a built venue *and* shape the direction of the field.

An analysis of built venues and precedents, the contexts of built forms, should inspire rather than fetter vital design. As the poet and critic T. S. Eliot wrote, "If the only form of tradition, of handing down, consisted in following the ways of the immediate generation before us in a blind or timid adherence to its success, 'tradition' should be positively discouraged."[10] These contexts of others' works should not be followed like fashion cycles or binding regulation, but rather as material for informed inspiration.

▶▶   *Study local built venues and global precedents for a
        project. Learn from, seek inspiration from, and judge
        your own work in light of both bodies of work.*

Street in the Stapleton neighborhood, Denver. The designers carefully referenced middle-class neighborhood patterns, building types, and iconic details of early-twentieth-century small towns.

Public Space

▶   To what public spaces can your project contribute?

Our places of conviviality—Main Street, town parks, public docks, sidewalks, swimming holes, and even grocery parking lots and fast-food hangouts—are essential to the life of a settlement. Here is where we run into friends, exercise the rights of assembly and free speech, display art, hold community parties and vigils, make memorials, play, and people-watch.

Like districts and towns, these places are often collectively designed. The spatial character of a street emerges, for example, from the interactions of buildings, sidewalks, roadways, utility infrastructure, public art, lighting, and other built forms. Some places may be just emerging or partially eroded and in need of design definition. Others may be vibrant but easily weakened.

Sometimes there are multiple convivial spaces overlapping and nested within one another. As a case in point, the Santa Monica Pier in Southern California defines a place that is the pier itself but that also allows people to be in the space of Santa Monica Bay, and it serves as the endpoint of Colorado Avenue and the historic Route 66. Likewise, the contexts for a bus stop shelter include its immediate site, the bus route, and the bus system.

Strong public rooms usually have a "stage" and an "auditorium": a central area where events happen and a surrounding field where people hang out and watch.

Plaza de los Héroes, La Paz, Bolivia. Great public spaces provide a venue for the political, social, and symbolic life of a community, and they are often composed by the concinnity of multiple built forms.

For instance the ice rink in Rockefeller Plaza, New York, is the stage, and the plaza hosts spectators. The ocean is a stage for Miami Beach, but the beach also has substages. Lifeguard stations are stages. Sunbathers create a show for the flow of pedestrians, and the pedestrians are on stage for the sunbathers.

Formal and informal uses of public spaces should be reviewed. Could a redesign better support these uses? Maybe a pavement pattern could establish locations for street market stalls, or an artwork could mark the starting point of a parade or guide the flow of pedestrians. Perhaps a building entry could serve as an informal stage for street musicians or shelter people waiting at a bus stop.

Formally, public rooms can be seen as composed of a floor, walls, furniture, and an implied ceiling that together define a sense of permeable enclosure akin to a soap bubble or a pool of light. Analyzing these parts and their collective gestalt (the form that is more than the sum of the parts) can suggest how a project might add to the space. For example, an architect remodeling a facade should understand the implications if all the neighboring buildings enclosing a square are white, and designers of utility lines should consider the height of the lines in relationship to the ceiling implied by tree canopies or building cornices. Analysis should look for weaknesses where new projects could provide more active edges, transform pavements into gracious floors, evoke a sense of ceiling, add missing furniture, and otherwise enrich the gestalt of the public space in question.[11]

▶▶ *Study the social practices and built forms of existing, emerging, fragmented, and potential public spaces.*

The lights over Denver's Larimer Street are an implied ceiling that makes this public space distinctive.

Design Domains

▶   How do we define the scope of design fields, and how do they interact and condition one another?

A tree is typically a single organism, but it also contributes to the health and character of a forest. It provides habitats for birds and constitutes the landscape of life for insects and lichens. Likewise, a built form is part of larger forms and a site for smaller forms.

Different design professions work at different levels. For example, interior designers work within building shells designed by architects who, in turn, work within an urban designer's layout of blocks and streets. The rules of these levels change from place to place and over time. In some settlements it is assumed that buildings may overhang a sidewalk, and in others, permission must be granted. The configuration of these levels can be a fundamental design decision. When do architects place buildings *in* landscapes versus landscape architects placing designs *around* buildings?

Different levels have different legal mechanisms and relationships to users. They also have different rates of change and replacement, and requirements for adaptability. For example, a plat for a nineteenth-century western U.S. railroad town outlining streets, blocks, parcels, and squares was primarily a legal real-estate document created by a corporation. The physical forms thus outlined have proved quite durable. The initial false-front commercial buildings in these communities, on the other hand, were designed primarily by carpenters and for the most part have not lasted as long.

The writer Stewart Brand describes six layers of buildings: site, structure, skin, services, space plan, and stuff.[12] Site normally is the most enduring, and frames the more ephemeral layers. The stuff—the occupants' furniture and belongings—typically is the most adaptable. This pattern may be different in some situations. Historic preservationists may value a facade (skin) more than a structure, and holy relics (stuff) may be more important than any other part of a structure housing them. However, Brand's hierarchy often holds true. It is critical to understand what belongs to each layer. Storefronts on major streets, for example, frequently change when new businesses inhabit the building. Therefore storefronts should be, and typically are, building skins that can be changed without rebuilding the structural system.

Balcony in Nicosia, Cyprus, extending into the fina. The ancient Levant convention of the fina is a zone along the street wall of a building in which balconies, downspouts, entry steps, and other features may protrude as long as they do not impede horse- or camelback riders or other users of the street. Typically, permanent protrusions must allow a given clearance. In many places, the building owner has rights to this space, including the ability to rent it to street vendors.

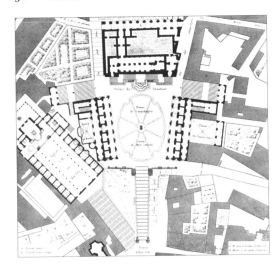

Piazza del Campidoglio by Michelangelo, from *Hegemann and Peets*, 1922.

Brand's layers can be expanded beyond a single building. At least in the modern West, parcels frequently outlast buildings. Blocks are more durable than the plots within them. A district's pattern of streets and blocks is more persistent than individual blocks or streets, and typically the underlying topography outlasts and influences the composition of districts. This hierarchy can help inform the design of a new building. For example, we can assume that a building is more likely to expand into neighboring lots than into the street, and thus we should place potential hallway connections alongside lot lines. Similarly, the success of a storefront along a window-shopping street is tied to the health of the district and should seek to support the street's character.

A strong designer will understand how more permanent layers condition and frame a project, and how the project in turn sets conditions for more changeable layers. Designing a bedroom so that its furniture can be well arranged in multiple patterns shows care for a more frequently adjusted layer. Designing the facade of a building on a square so as to help create the walls of the public room is an example of participating in the larger layers. In addition, projects can *redefine* bigger layers. Commissioned by Pope Paul III, Michelangelo's design for the Piazza del Campidoglio (1536–46) in Rome reoriented the Capitoline Hill district, Rome's historic civic center, away from the Roman Forum and toward Saint Peter's Basilica.

▶▶   *Master the design levels in which your project operates, and contribute to smaller and larger levels.*

Political-Economic Sectors

▶   How do political-economic sectors shape civil composition?

The powers, goals, and practices of three political-economic sectors—governments, markets, and nonprofit organizations—decisively shape civil design. A full introduction is beyond the scope of this book, as the distribution of powers and details of practices vary in numerous important ways. However, an outline of general issues for investigation follows.

Governments

Governments regulate, provide information, define property rights and types of ownership, tax, make public investments, establish due process, judge disputes, and seek agreements. Civil designers tend to focus on regulation, in the form of building and zoning codes. However, other governmental powers can be key aspects of context. For example, development of transferable air rights has significantly shaped downtowns, and the U.S. tax code is a major tool for historic preservation.

Civil designers not only work within these regulations and policies but also work out their detailed consequences and explore conflicts between rules. The Parisian mansard roof is a response to a tax on the number of floors below the roof. Likewise, "wafer" houses were developed to occupy narrow lots left over from early platting practices.

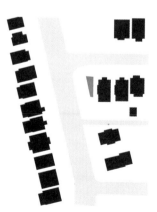

Plaque in New Orleans honoring the politicians who enabled extensive repairs to sidewalks.

"Wafer" house in Seattle, Washington. The intersection of a standardized platting plan with a differently oriented road or other platting grid generates a small triangular lot, as in the case of this house. The shape of the lot constrains possible building forms.

Markets

From design fee structures to banking practices, market practices drive design decisions. The following are some of modern markets' underlying conventions, which significantly influence composition but may not be immediately evident.

The products of global real estate practices, such as Wall Street–tradable project types and corporate franchise models, strongly respond to the standardizing context of the global market.[13] Essentially, these markets need uniform commodities to ease trading. To achieve this, they typically either minimize responses to other contexts (e.g., chain stores), or package a stock product in local dress (e.g., "Colonial" shopping malls) to the detriment of vital civil composition.

A partially countervailing trend is the concept of "investment grade design," or projects in which the benefits of high-quality design are likely to more than repay their costs. This should cover all good design. In practice, however, the concept is frequently associated with big-name signature projects. Thus this business practice can engender the creation of collectable built baubles that rely on their own idiosyncrasy.

In *The Culture of Building* (2000), Howard Davis discusses the spatial distribution of value within built forms. He shows that we spend varying amounts of money and design attention on different parts of our built forms. For example, in traditional urban buildings, more resources are devoted to elaborate street facades than party walls, and in twentieth-century suburbia, money is often spent on traffic lights and not sidewalks. These decisions may be driven by a convention of supporting the commonwealth (e.g., elegant street facades), or, as was frequent in the late twentieth century, an individualized cost-benefit analysis (e.g., the separate parking lots of strip-mall stores).

Practices of managing economic risk also shape building practices. The economic risk of constructing a built form demands a high interest rate on construction loans. This high rate, in turn, creates a growing tendency to speed construction by using as much premanufactured work as possible. Market risk can also induce concern about unproven styles, types, locations, and designers. Real estate practices can exacerbate the effects of this risk. For example, in some markets only buildings that have been constructed recently can serve as evidence of the viability of a project to secure a loan. Thus it can be hard to get a loan to construct building types such as apartments over retail if no one has built one recently, even if older examples have remained in profitable use for decades.

Even the way costs and benefits are defined and measured can shape composition. Categories of expenses and benefits include:

INITIAL COST: The purchase and installation price.

LIFE-CYCLE COST: The initial cost plus maintenance, insurance, operating, recycling, and other costs over the life of a built form. Using life-cycle rather than initial costs can help value durability, adaptability, and a good fit with the context. Life cycle can be conceived of in different ways. Some projects are evaluated over the life of the mortgage. Others consider the expected life of the built form.

SUNK COSTS: Funds already spent that cannot easily be recovered. Venues and individual built forms often persist because of sunk costs. For example, the mountain roads and building stock of the original mining town of Telluride, Colorado, provided grounds for the emergence of the contemporary ski town.

OPPORTUNITY COST: If a parking lot is placed in front of a shop, the opportunity of continuing an adjacent window-shopping sidewalk is lost. Any design replaces alternative dreams. When two different parties are interested in mutually exclusive alternatives, one will lose; thus opportunity costs can generate political conflicts.

EXTERNAL COST: A design may impose costs on, or give benefits to, neighbors that are not accounted for or even recognized by the builders. For example, a subdivision may interrupt a wildlife corridor.

VENUE COST: This is a particular type of external cost. Naturally, the venue can sometimes provide benefits, too. For example, individual stores gain from together making a window-shopping street and share the losses imposed by a drive-in in their midst. Backyard fruit trees benefit from bees and neighboring cross-pollinating trees but suffer the costs of widespread infestations.

Costs are not measured only in money. It is also important to examine social, professional, and political capital—the costs and benefits of an action to our trustworthiness, status, and inspirational power.

Understanding these costs helps illuminate the motives and actions of different stakeholders. Neighbors, for example, may be concerned about decisions that, to the project owner, are external costs. A business association may strongly support street landscaping because the members believe the improvement will benefit business. Moreover, projects can be shaped to respond to different conceptions of costs and benefits. An owner who sees the full life cycle of her building may invest in a more durable structure and in more adaptable parts than if she focuses on initial cost.

The Third Sector—Nonprofit and Community Organizations

Just as the American Civil Liberties Union defends civil liberties and the Robert Wood Johnson Foundation works to improve public health, third sector practice can promote the collective goods of civil composition. A few examples are the National Trust for Historic Preservation, Project for Public Spaces, and the Trust for Public Land.

Nonprofits exist to promote a public benefit. The United States and other nations' tax codes require an explicit statement of these goals. As professionals, civil designers are responsible to a set of collective goods. Thus many nonprofits may be natural allies of civil designers. The United Kingdom's Landmark Trust, for example, restores buildings and grounds as working parts of cultural landscapes.

Nonprofits and foundations may directly support or commission a design or an aspect of a design. In addition they may invest their endowment's "gradual money" (money that can wait longer for a return than with commercial lenders or can be invested in small increments over time).[14] They also offer faster action than governments, research and technical support, access to stakeholders, and organizational capacity. In the early twentieth century the Municipal Art Society of New York, for example, launched a campaign for "useful art" and produced designs for street signs and other street furniture, thus helping design New York's streets.[15]

Nonprofits may focus on projects, communities, or subject areas. The Central Park Conservancy supports New York City's Central Park; community foundations support nonprofits and groups within specified geographical areas; organizations such as the Nature Conservancy focus on ecosystems.

The third sector is often overlooked as a player in civil composition. With good knowledge of the field, there is ample opportunity for partnership and innovation.

▶▶ *Understand the effect of governmental powers, the structure of the market, and the possibilities of the third sector on individual projects.*

Tectonic Markets

▶   How might markets for materials, building
technologies, and craftspeople influence,
and in turn be shaped by, civil composition?

Whitewashed Greek hill towns and cedar-planked Northwest
American Indian settlements have a coherence that is largely
due to the cohesive palette of local materials and craft.
However, local building markets can change. The iconic metal
roofs of northern New Mexico emerged with the arrival of
the railroad and affordable access to suppliers. Likewise
the riot of materials in late-twentieth-century developments
reflects the increasing availability of choice. Local tectonics,
the art and practices of construction, clearly shape a venue's
built form.

Given that we have access to a wide range of materials,
how should we use materials and construction knowledge?
One mode is through planning policy. In 1918 the first British
military governor of Jerusalem, Sir Ronald Storrs, enacted
a bylaw requiring that Jerusalem stone be used for external
walls of all new buildings in the city. This material code, still
in force, mandates a continuity of appearance and visually
defines the geographic limits of the city.

Incentives can also shape material use. The Leadership
in Energy and Environmental Design (LEED) rating system
gives credits for the use of materials from within a five-
hundred-mile radius. This incentive can reduce the energy
costs of delivering materials and also sets the palette of
materials. To comply with the system, Texas limestone could
only be used in or near Texas, and Italian marble would not
be found in Napa, California.

The five-hundred-mile limit, however, is a crude
definition of a tectonic market area. Adjacency to a port,
canal, or railroad can reduce transport-energy costs and
reshape markets. For example, used shipping containers can
be purchased relatively inexpensively at ports and used to
frame small buildings. Environmental or other contexts may
suggest limits to the use of materials. The Thorncrown Chapel
in Arkansas by the architect E. Fay Jones was built in 1980
of small-dimension lumber to limit the impact of moving
materials and equipment onto a delicate site.

Civil designers can help shape tectonic markets. Each
material and trade decision is a choice not only about the
built form but also about what quarries or forests, factories or

Kakopetria, Cyprus. Town
morphologies (e.g., building to
the street edge and overhanging
balconies) and building typologies
and tectonics (e.g., stone bases,
plastered adobe walls, and wood)
work together to create a pleasantly
coherent street and village.

workshops, and employment practices will be engaged. After studying the tectonic market context, civil designers can help shape it by using purchasing power, renegotiating relationships between designers and builders, and redesigning construction practices.

Large orders can reopen a product line, but the purchasing power of even a small project can be significant. Landscape architects, for example, can work with nurseries to strengthen a market for native species. Specifications and standards can influence the process of production, as in the

View of Volos and the Aegean from Makrinista, Greece. The stone shingles and chimneys are characteristic tectonics of Pelion mountain villages.

case of design firm Perkins + Will. The firm researched twenty-five harmful chemicals used in building products, and its website states, "Rather than use harmful products, we will seek out alternatives that protect our health and the health of future generations. It is our hope that this list will be a catalyst for marketplace change."[16]

Relationships and contracts between designers and builders can vary widely and can significantly influence the form of completed projects. Creating long-term collaborations with craftspeople, as the Italian architect Carlo Scarpa did with Veneto artisans, can enable our constructions to embody a conversation between artists. Public art programs, design-build teams, and emerging design and fabrication methods may allow a significant reintroduction of artisanal work within industrial production. In concert with guilds or master craftsmen, projects can be designed to reinvigorate historic or local building crafts, such as thatching or stone carving. The Cathedral Church of Saint John the Divine in New York (begun in 1892 and ongoing), for example, was built following traditional Gothic engineering, and its construction brought stonecutters from Europe to train local craftspeople. Additionally, projects can be designed to provide entry-level jobs, allow owner construction, or invite community participation. The Pomegranate Center organizes communities to design and build community gathering places, and, among a host of services, Architecture for Humanity provides local labor and skills training.[17]

There is a history of designers redesigning materials and construction methods. Frank Lloyd Wright designed new patterns of concrete block. Other civil designers have been deeply involved in developing solar heating and lighting techniques. Currently, firms such as KieranTimberlake, Greg Lynn FORM, and Morphosis are actively shaping new design and construction practices. Tectonic markets shape what we build, but, as with other contexts, civil designers can shape tectonic markets.

▶▶   *Examine how tectonic markets determine what can be built, how the manufacture of materials shapes settlements, and how what we build can in turn shape the markets.*

Dancing in the Street

▶   How can individual projects support community
spatial practices?

Street busking, ATM queues, parades, and other uses of space
shape the city. Good civil design will enable, form, and enrich
such practices in the public realm. While these practices are
each quite specific, they fall into general categories. Dancing
the *sardana* in front of Barcelona's cathedral or dressing
up guinea pigs for a festival in Huacho, Peru, are practices that
are rich in specific details, but they also fall under the broader
category of public celebration. Following are categories of
spatial practices whose local manifestations should be studied.

COOPERATIVE MOBILITY: The complex set of interactions
between pedestrians, car drivers, bicycle messengers,
etcetera.[18] To provide appropriate stages and props for this
dance, designers must understand the nuances of its choreography. Walking itself is an exquisitely expressive act. More
than five pages of the *Oxford English Dictionary* are devoted to
the word *walk*. People hike, march, and trudge. They toddle
and shuffle. They parade, stroll, and saunter. Thus we should
provide more than a walking "lane" equivalent to a driving
lane. Window-shopping, for example, requires a length of
well-staged windows and a comfortable sidewalk. As the
Romans with their triumphal arches knew, a grand parade
route supports a grand parade. When we mix pedestrians
with people sitting, cars, bikes, and others, a complex system
emerges. Civil designers should seek to gracefully fit their
projects into and fine-tune this system—for example, by
providing space for bicycle parking near a main entrance
but far enough away to minimize conflicts with pedestrians,
placing entrances to toddler playgrounds away from busy
streets, or designing pedestrian-bicycle paths that connect
the ends of cul-de-sacs to adjacent routes.

SEEING AND BEING SEEN: One of the delights of being in
public is people-watching and occasionally putting yourself
on stage. Studies show that most of the time people hang out at
the edges of public spaces, taking the role of audience members watching the flow of pedestrians or activities in the center
of the space.[19] Therefore, creating good places to socialize,
such as street cafés, along the edges of plazas, streets, and other
public spaces is critical. Both formal and unmarked stages are
also important, however. An unmarked stage allows the fiction
that an actor is not purposely on stage. Well-designed doorways

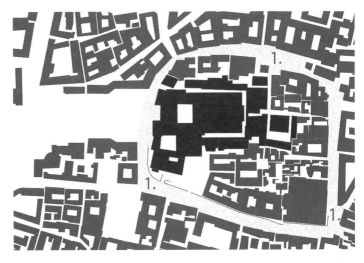

Diagram of a portion of Lhasa, Tibet, showing the Barkor (stippled street) encircling the Jokhang temple complex (darker figure). In Tibetan Buddhism, it is auspicious to make clockwise circumambulations of sacred sites. Routes created by pilgrims walking around a site are called *koras*. The Barkor, one of the koras around the temple, is a main market area. Koras are major components of Lhasa's morphology but have changed in form over time. The current shape of the Barkor was probably formed in the early 1900s.

Sardana dancers, Barcelona. This type of dance is a strongly place-based cultural practice, often done in plazas in front of Catalonian cathedrals, and associated with regional pride.

into a restaurant or theater lobby, for instance, may allow one to "make an entrance" while maintaining the fiction that one is simply entering the room.

PUBLIC CELEBRATION: The philosopher Karsten Harries wrote, "There is a continuing need for the creation of…places where individuals come together and affirm themselves as members of the community, as they join in public reenactments of the essential: celebrations of those central aspects of our life that maintain and give meaning to existence. The highest function of architecture remains what it has always been: to invite such festivals." [20] Built forms can directly support festivals: a town park can be designed as the terminus of a parade route, telephone poles can hold stage lights to illuminate street buskers, or a plaza can have a screen to show soccer matches. Built forms can also indirectly support festivity by, for example, providing great places to sit and watch street life, or celebrating stories of place.

TRIANGULATION: The urban researcher William H. Whyte coined the term *triangulation* to describe the phenomenon in which an activity or artwork provides the excuse for strangers to talk.[21] Artworks that prompt people to play, such as interactive fountains, are particularly effective at triangulation.

PLAY IN PUBLIC: Sidewalk hopscotch, chess in the park, charity runs, and the recent additions of parcour and flash mobs are part of the varied traditions of street theater and public play. Projects can enable these joyful spatial practices.

LEARNING BY LOOKING: The architect Louis I. Kahn wrote, "A city should be a place where a little boy walking through its streets can sense what he someday would like to be." [22] If a built form displays the activities it houses, the means of its construction, and the other systems it interacts with, then it can help educate. Such "pedagogic design" includes showing environmental processes (such as collecting rainwater) and people and machines at work.

PASSIVE SURVEILLANCE: The twentieth-century urbanist Jane Jacobs's famous term *eyes on the street* suggests that places where people easily see each other are more secure than hidden places.[23] This can work in multiple directions. If passersby can see into stores, they provide security because they can set off alarms or act as witnesses. Likewise, store clerks can observe the street. Public elevators and stairwells should be designed so that they are clearly seen from the street and neighboring buildings.[24]

LA RESOLANA: In northern New Mexico, *la resolana* (the place where the sun shines) is a warm south-facing wall where people gather to talk.[25] In Cyprus this same activity may happen under the tree of idleness.[26] The rights of free speech and assembly are rooted in protecting these practices. If a project will affect an existing rendezvous, it would be wise to consult with its regulars.

CIVIL SOCIETY AND POLITICAL ORGANIZING: One of the prime roles of the traditional town square is to host civil society and political groups. Petition signing, nonprofit advocacy, sports, festivals, and protests take place in the streets and parks. Projects can make space for these activities. For example, supermarket arcades may shelter diabetes awareness campaigns or pet adoptions. Parks could provide places for tai chi or community gardens.

Backgammon players, Nicosia, Cyprus. In many cultures, people play games in squares and other public places.

WRITING ON THE WALLS: As numerous examples preserved in Pompeii illustrate, graffiti is an ancient practice. This type of anonymous public speech is unlikely to disappear. Graffiti combines general considerations of public speech with issues of physical design. To evaluate graffiti, consider both its type of speech (e.g., gang markings, political commentary, artistic expression) and the form of its production (e.g., who owns the canvas, whether the work is permanent or temporary, the work's artistic merit). "Clean graffiti" is made by cleaning a message onto a public sidewalk, which is a much different act than spray painting a gang sign onto a store. Built forms can inhibit or promote graffiti. Smooth walls make a better canvas than rough surfaces do. Raw walls appear more likely to be tagged than facades that clearly show human craft and care.

► ► *Understand the social practices of a milieu, and, when possible, create built forms that enable appropriate practices or make them more pleasant.*

Gum wall, Post Alley, Seattle. Over the years people waiting in the theater line have added chewing-gum decorations to the wall. This multiauthor artwork/game is a source of social triangulation and public play.

Fictive Landscapes

▶   How should we design to respect, enrich, and
create storied places?[27]

As a species, we are storytellers—we imagine futures, give
meaning to our lives by retelling our experiences, and make
worlds from words. Storytelling may have been a critical
component of our evolution.[28]

Settlements materialize within a context of stories.
A city of feeling and meaning inhabits the city of fact, and
citizens will judge a project's fit with, or restructuring of, this
fictive landscape.[29] Ignorance of the fictive landscape is, at
a minimum, a lost opportunity. Frequently, disregard for the
stories of a place provokes community resistance to a project.
Moreover, this fabric can be a critical part of the sense of home
and belonging, and loss of this resource can, in egregious
cases like the so-called urban renewal of the 1960s, engender
a mental health crisis that impoverishes individuals and
destroys a community.[30]

Stories of place include published texts that take place
in the landscape, such as the Madeline series of children's
books by Ludwig Bemelmans set in Paris, the Eloise series by
Kay Thompson set in New York, or Tony Hillerman's books on
the Navajo Nation. The French philosopher Gaston Bachelard
explored how poetry and the spaces of home inform each
other.[31] Stories of place also include the customs of street
festivals, lover's lane's, and other practices (see "Dancing in
the Street" in this chapter); unbuilt and pending design
proposals that offer commentary and alternatives; and place
names that embody ways of life, such as the Left Bank (Paris),
Greenwich Village (New York), or Skid Row (Seattle).

Buildings, landscapes, public works, and other built
forms themselves embody aspects of narrative. They are, at
least, settings that frame and evoke stories. Generations of
students wear a path up stone steps. Windows are bricked
up, and attics are remodeled into penthouses. The faded
paint of old ads still graces sides of brick stores. These traces
tell everyday stories of a place. Even without leaving a legible
physical trace, our use of a place may imbue it with meaning.
For example, couples regularly choose to get married in the
old plazas of New Mexico. Later, when they or their guests
come to the plaza, they are reminded of the celebration. With
generations of weddings, the institution of marriage becomes
part of the spirit of the place.

Il Facchino fountain, Rome. The ca. 1580 fountain tells stories in at least two ways. It depicts a water vendor, like those who sold water during the previous century when Rome's fountains were in disrepair. Thus it spoke to the new era of public works. The fountain was also one of the "talking statues." For centuries, political satires, known as pasquinades, written by the Romans to ridicule the authorities, were attached to these fountains.

The author Jonathan Safran Foer reading outside the Shakespeare and Company bookstore in the Left Bank of Paris. The original store served as a gathering place for Lost Generation writers. The current store continues to be a center of the local literary scene.

Moreover, we design buildings and places to provide specific narrative settings. Gothic churches are meant to evoke the light of God's grace. Nineteenth- and early-twentieth-century U.S. post offices were intended to present the dignity of the federal government, and Prada stores aim to impart a branded prestige.

Artworks often evoke interactive place stories. *Rachel*, a life-size brass piggy bank at Pike Place Market in Seattle, attracts a steady stream of people to be photographed next to it, and the sculpture collects about $10,000 a year for charity. The gates to San Francisco's Chinatown declare that a distinct district lies beyond and suggests its characteristics.

We take photos of public artworks and iconic facades to help tell the story of our visit. These photo tales in turn eulogize their settings and help make a name for the place. Disney knows this and provides settings for snapshots at its parks, along with "Kodak points" that indicate the best place to take the photo. But promoting tourism is not the only role of Kodak points. Iconic artworks serve as landmarks in a community's conceptual maps, settings for TV news reports, rallying points for celebrations and protests, and points of triangulation— social prompts for strangers to talk. They are icons in the narrative fabric.

Strong stories outlast their authors. The tales are passed to heirs to restage or rewrite, and move between art forms. In his playful postmodern fantasy Discworld series, Terry Pratchett entertains an ornate version of this idea:

> People think that stories are shaped by people. In fact, it's the other way around. Stories exist independently of their players. If you know that, the knowledge is power. Stories, great flapping ribbons of shaped space-time, have been blowing and uncoiling around the universe since the beginning of time....This is called the theory of narrative causality and it means that a story, once started, *takes a shape*.[32]

Without postulating new forms of space-time, we can see that compelling place-stories are told, retold, and, like language itself, exist in the commons. The romance of Route 66 continues to inspire people to build riffs on Streamline Moderne, roadside kitsch, and pueblo deco. Across North America the idea of the New England village echoes through suburban developments, and the notion of "Main Street" continues to inspire political rhetoric and designs for rebuilding actual Main Streets.[33]

Cloud Gate by Anish Kapoor, Chicago, 2006. This is perhaps the ultimate Kodak point: It aids tourism, serves as a landmark, functions as a setting for TV news reports, and prompts strangers to talk and play in public.

This imperative to know the stories of a place favors civil designers who live and work in a region where, over time, they can deeply read the place. Nevertheless, active study can inform an outsider or give new perspectives to a local. Published fiction, histories, urban studies, historic postcards, maps, and other texts can provide a grounding. This can be focused with site analysis that includes a history of the built form and uses of the site and its neighborhood: Who built here before, why, and with what goals? However, both native and outside designers should also interview clients, users, and citizens to discover *their* stories of place (see "Community Consultation" in "Framing and Reframing").

These stories may directly influence built form. Catalonian and European tales, for example, are quite legible in a number of Antoni Gaudí's buildings. Thomas Jefferson and other contemporary architects used Roman styles for federal buildings expressly to associate the United States with Roman republicanism. The power of landscape architect Richard Haag's 1975 Gas Works Park in Seattle and Germany's Duisburg-Nord Landscape Park (1994), based on the designs of Peter Latz, is in their evocation of stories of industry, ruin, and rebirth.

▶▶   *Actively read a site's stories: the texts and artworks, spatial practices and traces, place names, public art and ornament, design types, patterns, and morphologies.*

Taste Cultures

▶   How can designers understand and respond to
the tastes of multiple audiences?

The meaning of *taste* in the sense of aesthetic judgment is
first recorded in John Milton's 1671 *Paradise Regained*.[34]
In the sixteenth century, the English humanist Sir Thomas
More gave us the sense of the word *culture* as the cultivation
of the mind through education and training.[35] In 1974 the
sociologist Herbert Gans coined the term *taste cultures* to talk
about how groups of people adopt a set of aesthetic standards
and values applied to a cluster of cultural forms.[36] Gans was
particularly interested in arguing that there can be multiple
well-founded taste cultures.

These adjacent buildings in New York
share massing, punched openings in
a mass wall, and other fundamental
characteristics, but differ in the tastes
expressed in their facades.

Different audiences for a built work frequently judge its aesthetics differently, in accordance with their taste cultures. For example, neighbors of a low-income clinic, the clinic's board of directors, and clinic patients most likely possess different criteria and judgments. Aspects of taste cultures can be subtle. I have found, for example, that compared to northerners, people native to the Sunbelt frequently underappreciate images with cloudy or foggy light.

To clearly understand taste cultures relevant to your project, look to three generally available sources of information: existing built form, market research, and conversations with stakeholders.

Investments that people have previously made in built form are guides to their aesthetic viewpoints. Walled subdivisions, for example, frequently also have regulations on building style and yard use. These rules enforce a strong taste for conformity and suggest that this community would prefer that a proposed neighboring clinic quietly blend in. However, care is needed in drawing conclusions from existing built form. A community may value conformity in houses, for instance, but embrace staged exoticism in a proposed restaurant. Moreover, built form represents past decisions; the community may have changed.

Market research also has its pros and cons. The consumer behavior research industry analyzes lifestyles, psychographics (e.g., interests, attitudes and opinions, social class, and brand loyalty), neighborhood type, media preferences, and spending habits to define systems of market segments, akin to taste cultures, that predict groups' interests in products and motivations to buy. The Nielsen Claritas system, for example, identifies segments such as "Young Digerati," who live in trendy mixed-use urban fringe neighborhoods and, as a whole, exhibit certain preferences. However, market segmentation can be a destructively self-fulfilling tool. For example, when banks redline a district, indicating places in which they will not make loans or will charge high interest rates, they further discourage other forms of investment in the district.

Market research can be conducted at various levels of detail. Typically only large subdivision builders, retail chains, high-end condominium developers, and others with a large customer base can afford comprehensive market segmentation research. Many projects use more targeted market research focusing on specific questions, such as what styles appeal to purchasers of lofts in a specific market. Quick-and-dirty market research can be conducted by reviewing census data, studying local grocery stores and other retailers to see which markets they cater to, and walking through a neighborhood noting market indicators such as children's toys or the age and type of parked cars.

Built form and market analysis, however, are indirect and generalized. They can readily reinforce stereotypes and suppress change. Their best use may be to prepare for discussions with stakeholders. Based on this research, designers can develop questions and provide visual examples for discussion. Image-based discussions can focus a conversation on specific issues and possibilities. What features might communicate dignity and put clinic clients at ease? Could a walled garden parking court help the project fit into the neighborhood and provide privacy for clients? Well-conducted community consultation can yield nuance and clarity. It can allow people to discuss and integrate a whole set of factors, and possibly change their minds.

There is, however, another set of stakeholders: the designer, the firm, and the professions. As part of a professional culture, designers bring a shared body of knowledge; a way of seeing projects; and typical customs, such as a connoisseurship of pens and orienting drawings with north up. Reputations are shaped by how work appeals to design juries, potential employers and employees, and magazine editors.

The influence of this taste culture can make it difficult to hear and respond to others. Publishing your firm's design principles clarifies your approach to clients and others, and because your ground is established, it may be easier to see and understand others' positions.

Studying the thicket of taste cultures, however, is not the only approach to a community's aesthetics. A second strategy to balance a variety of tastes and desires is to find components of common ground. Research suggests that humans pervasively value access to nature, a sense of protected shelter (refuge) with a view (prospect), curved paths that suggest there is more to see just beyond (mystery), dynamic symmetry, filtered sunlight, evidence of care and craftsmanship (making special), and well-organized but multilayered spaces (ordered complexity).[37] This view of aesthetics argues that just as humans are hardwired for language, there are aspects of composition and landscape that are cross-culturally appealing but with cultural, social, and personal variations.[38]

Understanding taste cultures and specieswide preferences does not imply that a designer should blindly follow the context of tastes. Rather, this knowledge can serve as a basis for aesthetic leadership. The leadership of taste-making comes in multiple forms. For example, Jimmy Cliff made me love reggae, a musical taste culture previously unknown to me, and Emmylou Harris allows me to transcend my lack of appreciation for country music. In both cases, their leadership rests on a deep understanding and love of their genres.

►►   *Research and represent the tastes of the various stakeholders, including those of yourself, your firm, and your profession. Search for approaches that are multivalent, synthetic, and rich.*

* * *

This outline of contexts may appear overwhelming, yet this list by no means exhausts the realm of potentially significant contexts. Endemic diseases and infectious pathways, patterns of environmental justice, organizational structures and missions of design firms, and the migration routes of elephants are other contexts that could figure into a design. Each of these contexts is a field of study in itself, and it is not feasible for a designer to conduct a thorough, independent study of every single context for each project.

Fortunately, built venues are rich with useful information and examples, because they embody previous designers' struggles with the myriad contexts. Moreover, as the following chapter outlines, built-form types also offer first approximations of informed contextual responses.

A habit of regular research, an understanding of traditions of built forms, talking with community members, and an abiding interest in places and communities will, with time, result in expert knowledge. Civil designers know places.

Built Species

Symbionts
Public Works
Naturalizing Clones
Life Stages

Built Species

> Could it be that the space of the finest cities came into being after the fashion of plants and flowers in a garden—after the fashion, in other words, of works of nature, just as unique as they, albeit fashioned by highly civilized people?
> —Henri Lefebvre

Lighthouse near Oban, Scotland. Lighthouses are by necessity enmeshed in their environments, but all built forms have roles to play in the larger context.

In urban composition, as in chess, the meaning of a move is dependent on the rules of the game, the context made by other pieces, *and* the characteristics of the piece. "Built species," the game pieces, are lineages or traditions handed down over time because an association between a built form and social practices retains cultural coherence, utility, and meaning. Courthouse squares, shopping mall storefronts, boulevards, and brownstones are all examples of built species. Understanding the characteristics of lineages is vital for civil composition because communities understand, value, and invest meaning in them, and because they embody a long history of design thought about how to house programs well within a confluence of contexts. (An architectural "program" is the set of intended activities and the spatial characteristics supporting those uses.)

I propose the term *species* rather than *type* because it suggests that these are lineages, not ahistorical truths, and it prompts examination of the robust fields of evolutionary theory and complex adaptive systems for useful concepts. There is no ideal courthouse square, only a population of squares that share a range of traits. These characteristics can change over time as social practices alter. The American suburban house, for example, has significantly increased in size since World War II, and the typical home garage underwent a few generations of transformation in location, size, function, and meaning during the twentieth century.[1]

French dwelling house, from *Harper's Weekly*, November 20, 1907. This sixteenth-century house with a ground-floor stable was a precedent for automobile parking in urban residences.

Of course, unlike natural biological species, built-form species are shaped by humans. They are similar to dog breeds or organizations such as university departments, whose development is shaped by cultural selection—the myriad actions of multiple people in a complex, emergent manner that is not easily predicted.

Just as biologists do not define biological species simply by function (e.g., flyers, swimmers), built species are not simply categories of use (e.g., dwelling, office). Nor are they simply patterns of forms (e.g., courtyard building). Rather they are culturally recognized confluences of programs, spatial practices, built configuration, tectonics, and niche in a built venue. A traditional stone-domed Turkish community well, for example, provides water, serves as a memorial to the benefactor who built the well, and offers a focal point and gathering place for a neighborhood. Roundabouts, public rose gardens, and craftsman bungalows developed through their own confluences of factors.

The species in a cultural landscape may evolve slowly from changes in tastes and cultural forms, or dramatically during a cultural shift or "invasion" from another cultural landscape (see "Cultural Shifts" in "Framing and Reframing"). Suburban invasions of farmlands, for example, replace one ecosystem of species with those of another cultural landscape. In these transformations, difficult adjacencies often arise, such as a housing tract next to a pig farm.

This chapter explores three categories of built species and their life stages. Symbionts are built forms that "live together" and shape one another's habitats. Public works are hosts that create habitats or contexts for other species. Naturalized clones are mass-produced products of industrial design, such as lampposts and mobile homes, that have been adapted to specific contexts. Finally, built species have various lifespans and life stages.

Community well, Nicosia, Cyprus. The well not only provides water but also is the formal focal point of pedestrian streets and the social gathering place for this neighborhood. A neighbor is using the solid top of the well to air household rugs.

Symbionts

▶   How can built species collectively
create resilient and vital built venues?

A project's role can be understood from different perspectives.
A business owner is likely to see a building primarily as a tool
for her business. A contractor values the opportunity to build it
and then to market its quality. The bank will value the building
as an economic commodity that can be sold for another use
in case the business fails. The district business association
will desire a business and building that support the character
and vitality of the area. Neighboring homeowners may want
a vital business, minimal disturbance to their domestic milieu,
and a sense of place.

Built species emerge from the interplay of these
explicit goals as well as the players' unexamined assumptions
and predictions. Thus it is difficult to invent a wholly new
built species. There must be a coming together of cultural,
economic, political, technological, and design intentions, often
driven by some cultural shift that demands a renegotiation
of our conventions.

Prize-winning entry by Martin
Beck for a student competition for
"aeroplane landing in a metropolis,"
from *American City Magazine,*
February 1926. Such inventions of
new, built species can help promote
discussion. However, to become
more than ideas they must embody
a confluence of cultural, economic,
political, and technological intentions.

On most occasions, designers work with established built species, modifying them to fit particular circumstances. There is as much creative possibility in this work as in breeding new species. In fact, freed by the economic, social, and political conventions embodied in a type, urban designers can concentrate on spatial and tectonic development. For instance, rather than spending time proving to bankers the economic viability of the *concept* of townhouses over shops, effort can be focused on the form of the particular project.

With well-established built species, projects can be simple and elegant, provide for the initial program, and fit gracefully into a built landscape. The built species harmonizes with its contexts. Often it would be a loss to attempt a radical reinvention. Professional organizations should give awards for these well-crafted "fabric" projects, and students should attempt these projects first.

A cluster of apartment buildings in Rome. Like a closely packed grove of trees, these buildings have grown into one another.

Built species play particular parts within a built venue; the vitality of a project depends on deeply understanding how built forms are *symbiotic* (from the Greek term for "live together"). Typically a restaurant has a better chance of success on a street that develops an active nightlife than on a quiet street. Use of a playground depends on ease and safety of access from surrounding neighborhoods. A good window-shopping sidewalk depends on both economic and physical synergy—the buildings must collectively make the display wall. Bookstores, inexpensive restaurants, and rental housing congregate near universities, and good collective design will create a *place* like Harvard Square or Oxford's Carfax out of this aggregation. This observation is embodied in the biological concept of niche, a particular role and position in the environment to which a species is well suited. A niche describes how a species "makes a living" in an environment and how it in turn alters the environment.

Some aspects of the environment are critical to a species, some minor, and others trivial. High traffic counts, for example, may be advantageous for a gas station but harmful for a home. Active nightlife may be the lifeblood of a British high street but trouble for an American "Elm Street." The concept of niche-perspective, the way a species values the environment, can help designers define the critical contexts for a project. Where have others of this type succeeded? What contexts are nurturing, and how can context problems be minimized or recast?

Good gardeners create a fit between site and species by choosing favorable sites for a species, modifying sites to better

right

The so-called block of discord, Barcelona. Although the three neighboring buildings by early modern masters are in disparate styles, together they form a portion of the street wall conforming to the urban design patterns of the Eixample district. The facades are all decorated mass walls of similar height, composed with elaborated bases, middles, and tops. The windows of all three are punched openings with highly structured frames. Moreover, they share the goal of creating public masks displaying wealth and cultural status.

below

Because it has streets on two sides, the end unit of this set of townhouses in San Diego occupies a different condition than those in the middle of the row, and its design was modified to take advantage of the condition and add interest to the composition.

suit a plant, and adapting species to given sites. Similarly, for civil designers, site selection involves searching for favorable economic, real estate, and design factors; design can transform the viability of a site, and designers continually modify types to take advantage of specific contexts.

While respecting the balance of interests embodied in a built species, designers should avoid lifeless replication of "the rules." There are no absolute ideal characteristics of a species, and each site offers unique opportunities. Developing rich responses to the web of contexts creates better individual projects, builds knowledge about how built species can adapt to changing contexts, and strengthens the larger systems of which the project is a component. There are a number of misconceptions that keep us from attaining rich responses.

We sometimes oversimplify by assuming that a project can only either conform or be novel. Gaudí's 1912 Casa Milà apartment building in Barcelona is widely understood as a novel building. However, it conforms to the urban design rules of the Catalan urban planner Ildefonso Cerdá's Eixample district and thus does its part in constructing a continuous street wall with balcony projections. Even the Manzana de la Discordia (block of discord), on which three disparate modernist buildings—Gaudí's 1877 Casa Batlló, the architect Josep Puig i Cadafalch's 1900 medieval Dutch–inspired Casa Amatller, and the architect Lluís Domènech i Montaner's 1902 Casa Lleó Morera—sit side by side has a remarkable coherence and helps make the fabric of Barcelona.

Sometimes designers think of the program of a project as a given, outside of the realm of design. However, shaping a built form's program can be key to civil composition. Even the program of national chain stores varies according to context. For example, despite the strong pattern of limited entrances, some supermarkets in dense settings place the florist, deli, or other departments on the front facade and provide them with windows and a separate door, creating a set of semi-independent storefront shops. Tailoring programs to a place should be part of a designer's brief. This, of course, must be done in detailed dialogue with the proprietors and with a robust understanding of the "program of place."

The program of place is the milieu's set of uses and their spatial characteristics. Window-shopping sidewalks, a ballpark's after-game restaurant district, and the route of a Mardi Gras parade embody programs of place. Detailed analysis of this program can be critical. For instance, stretching a strolling realm a block further to reach your site requires understanding what currently defines the limits of the strolling district: Is the district lit differently? Does a building, park, or statue serve as a terminus? Do the buildings help create a great sidewalk, or does the topography distinctly change?

There are "orphan" built species—unglamorous projects in which designers have not invested their best efforts. The gas station/convenience store, for example, could adapt to better fit walking districts. Downspouts could be reconceived as water harvesting devices and artworks, and, as I have argued elsewhere, the parking lot should be rethought to better support pedestrians, be more environmentally responsible, and support conviviality.[2]

Sometimes we dismiss the potential power of small projects. The Seattle coffee boom arose not only from Starbucks and brethren cafes but also from pioneering sidewalk coffee carts. Development of this small built form provided low-capital entry into the market and enlivened Seattle's street scene. Similarly, New York's community gardens are credited with transforming the character of neighborhoods.[3]

Finally, there is the issue of parasites: projects that benefit from a built venue but weaken it. Three questions may help determine if a project is parasitic. Does the power of the design depend on being an exception that others must be kept from using, for example, capturing views and attention by being taller than surrounding buildings? If so, would others agree that there is a good reason for your project's exception? Secondly, can you draw larger built patterns that the design supports and enriches? Thirdly, do the critical parts of the project support collective goods, as defined by the community, such as public health?

▶▶   *Built species have been designed to both fit and help shape cultural landscapes. Match the built species to the niche offered by the site. Design the site to best support the project, and adapt the species to the nuances of the site's multiple contexts.*

Downspout Garden by Buster Simpson, Seattle, 1999. Designers can rethink established patterns of built form, particularly "unglamorous" forms such as parking lots or power substations, to create delight or other public benefits.

Detail of a street in Portland, Oregon, providing water detention and filtering.

Sidewalk pavement pattern in Barcelona. A kind of cultural infrastructure is created by the use of this pattern throughout the city. It marks the extents of the city's grounds and is used as an icon on posters and T-shirts to evoke Barcelona's street life.

Public Works

▶   How might designers of public works help compose settlements?

Most projects are hosts for other built forms, and thus, like nurse logs, should provide good environments for these projects. Cabinet makers and kitchen designers work within houses, and neighborhood parks are the sites for playground designers' work. Moreover, this book argues that all projects should support collective goods and compose larger systems. In this sense, all projects are partially public works.

Public works, however, have a principal goal of providing a collective good or service to a catchment or district. Typically, these public built forms also provide a spatial framework and opportune sites to host associated projects. Streets, for example, provide access, but they also organize blocks and are places themselves that host adjoining facades, street furniture, street trees, parks, telephone lines, and other systems.

The range and types of collective goods and services provided by public works are a matter of politics, but designers may help make the case for various types of public works. In the development of the renowned public art master plan for Phoenix, the urbanists Catherine Brown and William Morrish identified a "cultural infrastructure" composed of historic urban patterns, the urban terrain (the juncture of landform and urban patterns), and the public cognitive map (the landmarks, borders, and territories that make the perceived structure of the city). Public art, they proposed, could illuminate, support, and compose this infrastructure "that we thought was as important to residents' sense of security, comfort, and belonging as are heat and light." [4]

Some collective goods, such as public health and fire protection, are regularly provided by a government. Others, such as electricity, are often supplied by regulated monopolies or government-owned utilities. The form of the organization can limit flexibility in defining the scope of the collective good and responding to opportunities. Some U.S. courts, for example, have greatly limited the ability of municipal corporations to commission public art. The Superior Court of Washington wrote, "[Seattle] City Light may not spend utility funds for the purpose of mitigating a substation's appearance, when the primary purpose of the art is to provide artistic benefit to the surrounding neighborhood and the public as a whole." [5] Apparently ratepayers can erect an ugly substation that damages neighborhood property values but cannot mitigate this with artwork.

A public work's catchment or service area directly affects both the siting and form of facilities and larger aspects of urban composition. Utility service boundaries, for example, have been used to limit sprawl. Being within the walls of a city once defined a distinct way of life.

Within their service areas, public works frequently provide a spatial framework that may be used to structure a district. Irrigation canals may become pedestrian greenways. Power line corridors may provide an edge to a neighborhood. In their heyday, streetcar stops prompted development of neighborhood commercial nodes.[6] The ordering principles of the network are typically reflected in the spatial urban framework. Centralized networks, such as town wells, spin out starlike paths. Distributed systems, such as building-based solar power, encourage meshlike patterns. Thus, by providing a public utility and structuring a district, public works create a pattern of niches for various built species.

In the twentieth century there was a shift from building "public works" to creating "infrastructure." While this semantic change emphasizes the network over the single-project aspect of the work, it also marks a set of practices that have been detrimental to flourishing urban composition.

Infrastructure design after World War II had a strong tendency toward nearly monofunctional solutions. Main streets were designed to move the maximum number of vehicles and became poor places for pedestrians and parades. Likewise, telephone poles were just poles, and great effort was devoted to suppressing their use as notice boards or bird nests.

Water tank and public observation tower at Volunteer Park, Seattle, from *American City Magazine*, May 1915.

Infrastructure has also typically been composed of generic parts. The metal benches placed in most of New Mexico's plazas in the late twentieth century are clones. Nineteenth-century railroad surveyors platted towns with nearly identical grids and street names.[7] The water tower in Seattle's Volunteer Park, on the other hand, illustrates the multifunctional public works approach. The Olmsted brothers, designers of the park, worked with the water authority so that, in addition to providing water storage and pressure, the tower provides a public observation point from the top of the hill, creates a visual terminus to Millionaires' Row (a street of expensive homes), and makes an elegant entry into the park.

Of course, this public works approach requires balancing different agendas rather than maximizing a single goal (storing water), and when compared to the cost of a simpler water tank, the multiuse tank has higher construction costs. However, if we compare it to building a water tank, a separate observation tower, and a park entrance gate, then a single structure is less expensive. The opportunity costs of single-use structures are often left off balance sheets by advocates of monofunctional design.

As designers of individual parts of an infrastructure system, say a firehouse or cell phone tower, civil designers naturally must attend to requirements of the system but should also fit the project into other systems and contexts. Some of the most successful cell tower designs are not fake trees but towers that exist for other reasons, such as a church steeple or water tank. Constructed as artworks, perhaps, an array of cell towers could be wayfinding devices, entrance markers, and rendezvous points for a campus.

▶▶   *Understand and shape the catchment, spatial framework, and niches engendered by a public works project. Design multiuse built forms that effectively carry out their role within the service network and help compose the settlement. Reinterpret and enrich existing infrastructures.*

Dragon sculpture by Seattle Spiral, International District of Seattle, 2002. The ubiquitous telephone pole is reframed as a dragon perch, reinforcing a narrative of the district.

Naturalizing Clones

▶   How can we adapt standardized built forms to deftly
fit their contexts?

Built-form clones—such as telephone booths, portable
classrooms, premanufactured hotel rooms, standard
street designs, and regulation tennis courts—are mass-
produced products or the results of highly specific standards.
Clones often offer significant advantages, such as reduced
manufacturing costs, quality control, ease of maintenance and
repair, and familiarity of use. The uniformity of traffic signs
and official basketball courts is clearly beneficial. However,
characteristically clones are contextually mute.

    Are there strategies that allow the efficiencies of mass
production but also provide context benefits, such as fitting
with local climate and landforms, supporting community
identity, or offering user control? How may repetition become
a site-responsive variation on a theme? The following are
some possible strategies.

A collage of streetlamps, *Urban
Light* by Chris Burden, Los Angeles
County Museum, 2008.

VARIATIONS: Creating a system of variations to fit a variety of defined conditions allows more degrees of fit. In large and competitive markets, such as clothing, this approach can offer a wealth of variety. Smaller markets, like that for parking meters, are more limited. Variations can be created for a particular area, such as a gas-lamp district; a hierarchy of systems (neighborhood street lights versus arterial street lights); or other urban forms.

ADDITIONS: Local fit can be increased by providing a set of customizable parts, such as a selection of front porches for a tract house, or shades that can be placed on different parts of a bus stop shelter depending on its solar orientation. "Open" design that provides means to attach additions made by other manufacturers can increase possibilities for local adaptation.

INTERACTIVITY: The chair, as William H. Whyte documented, is preferable to the fixed bench because we can move it, adjusting it to the weather and the social climate.[8] Adjustable parts, writing surfaces, information provision, and other forms of interaction allow users to fit the clone to the context.

MULTIUSE: Understanding and accommodating the multiple uses to which a design will be put can help a clone fit into multiple contexts. For example, parking meters can have a step for tying shoes, provide a loop for leashing a dog, tell the time, or sell electricity to recharge cars. At the Massachusetts Institute of Technology (MIT), the Media Lab's Smart Cities group is developing augmented street lights that have multiple responsive actions, such as flashing red in front of a building where someone has called for an ambulance.

PLACEMENT PATTERNS: Developing criteria, patterns, and information for siting stock products may also improve site fit. Examples include a guide to placement of manufactured homes, or composing sidewalks so that lampposts and other street furniture form a "hedge" between a clear walking zone and the driving lanes. Developers could improve information available for purchasers customizing new houses (e.g., adding a bay window) by displaying the house plans on a three-dimensional model of the selected site that shows neighboring existing and proposed houses.

ENCAPSULATION: A standardized form may be placed within a larger setting that helps it fit into the context. A parking structure, for example, may be lined with small shops.

ICONS: A converse approach is occasionally powerful. Rather than adapting a product to contexts, create products that embody a context. The British telephone booth can evoke

right
A parking meter in the Rhyme and
Meter Project, Albuquerque, 1999.
The project paired artists with
poems and gave them parking
meters as canvases.

below
A shipping container house by
Ross Stevens, Wellington, New
Zealand, 2008. Reuse of materials
and structures is an ancient and
enduring practice. Romans and
Venetians, for example, often
reused stones.

England in the African bush—and probably on Mars. Moreover, sports and game courts create their own specific contexts. The rules of these contexts must be followed, but as the variety of chess boards demonstrates, there are ways to both conform and adapt.

A COLLAGE OF CLONES: A unique place can be constructed by combining multiple stock components in unique configurations or with site-specific components. The artist Chris Burden's *Urban Light* (2008), for example, is a field of vintage streetlights at the Los Angeles County Museum of Art.

MASS CUSTOMIZATION: Recent developments in manufacturing allow crafting of individual works with near assembly-line efficiencies.[9] If site-specific information is used to form or select individually crafted elements, stock designs may become site specific. Mobile homes, for example, may be customized for site-specific daylight, climate, and view conditions.

ON-SITE CUSTOMIZING: Clones can be treated as canvases. The car detailing industry can provide a model and, in some cases, the craft to customize industrial products. Albuquerque's Rhyme and Meter project, in which parking meters were decorated with poems and artwork, illustrates this approach.

REPURPOSING: Clones can be used for something other than their original purposes in ways that enrich the contexts. For example, designers have reused shipping containers for buildings.

License plate shingling in Telluride, Colorado. This follows an older practice by miners of using tin cans for shingles.

▶▶   *Search for systemic methods and individual opportunities to contextualize clones without losing their advantages.*

Life Stages

▶   What are the appropriate lifespan and life stages
for a project?

Burning Man, Black Rock City,
Nevada. This annual event in the
Nevada desert is a prime example
of a recurring form.

Some built forms are intended to be ephemeral, such as
a backyard wedding garden, *The Gates* (2005) by Christo and
Jeanne-Claude, or detour routes. Others, like the Burning
Man festival or farmers' markets, are recurrent perennials.
Most projects by civil designers, however, are intended to be
long-lived. These come in two categories. Traditionally, we
built durable forms that frequently had multiple life stages,
outlasting their founding program and their designers.
Recently, there has been a tendency to create structures that
depreciate over the life of the mortgage. Each of these lifespans
conditions the built form's role and way of evaluating contexts.

Ephemeral built forms often support the senses of
conviviality and genius loci. We play with the climate, discuss
and protest politics, share mourning, and express creativity
through ephemeral structures. Often these have very specific
contextual fits, such as you-had-to-be-there jokes. The spatial
tactics and built forms of protests (e.g., tent cities, barricades),
and the emerging practices of flash mobs and in situ theater
are, for example, often dependent on the moment and the site.
Yet, like other works of art, even these short-lived site-specific
projects may, if publicized, resonate in the larger culture. The
mode of appearance, duration, and departure are often central
compositional concerns. Andy Goldsworthy's *Midsummer
Snowballs* (2000), for instance, appeared overnight, and
Londoners enjoyed their melting away. In that case, all that was
left were photographs, but an ephemeral event designer may
propose to leave physical traces, souvenirs that endure. The
grounds and improvements of world's fairs and the Olympics
may be as valuable as the events.

Recurrent built forms, such as a Renaissance fair,
frequently have two components: the current installation,
and the grounds and traditions that sustain building new
installations. The installation may be an ephemeral form, or it
may attempt to embody some invariant type, like the Japanese
Ise shrine, which is rebuilt every twenty years. The fields frame
the installation and are durable forms.

Mortgage-life projects, such as many chain stores and
mobile homes, treat built forms like factory equipment. They
have a precisely defined function, a calculated lifetime, and, on
occasion, a decommissioning plan. This single-use approach is

Midsummer Snowballs by Andy Goldsworthy, London, 2000. This temporary artwork played on its own disappearance.

akin to ephemeral projects except that the fit with program and context must last longer, and thus some degree of adaptability is advisable.

Although a limited design life can reduce unnecessary monetary and environmental costs, this approach can also engender a set of problems. Due to the higher cost of construction loans and price competition in some markets, builders may be tempted to design "products" with low initial costs and poor life-cycle costs, which, in short order, they sell to users. This can create a false economy in which users and neighbors suffer. For example, slight increases in initial costs, such as improved insulation in mobile homes, can reduce both operating and environmental costs. If presented with the option, the user, the regional electric utility, or a housing advocacy group might be willing to pay the higher initial cost.

Moreover, this mortgage-life approach dismisses the possibility that built forms may gain value over time by adding to a larger milieu. Historic preservation efforts, adaptive reuse projects, and central metropolitan real estate prices argue that built forms can gain value from time and context.

Durable built forms require the means to adapt to changing contexts and programs. Designers should consider likely changes to program and context and test their designs against these scenarios.[10] If a restaurant fails, can it easily be sold for other retail uses? If the theater across the street reopens, can we attract their foot traffic? If a tree dies along a street, how will it be replaced and how will that affect the composition? If bicycle use increases, can neighborhood streets be easily connected to a trail along the power line corridor? The architect and professor John Habraken and open building advocates have explored various means to provide for adaptability at different design levels.[11]

We tend to change different domains of building systems at different rates (see "Design Domains" in "Contexts"). Functionally separating these layers aids adaptability so that, for example, playground equipment can be changed without rebuilding the park in which the equipment sits.

Providing spatial slack, a bit of extra space at critical junctures and edges, can ease repairs, renovations, or other uses. Freeway shoulders, for example, allow accident removal and lane repairs. A stream's riparian zone allows for floods, repositioning of the stream bed, and wildlife movement.

Finally, programming from context suggests thinking of potential uses of a built form from the point of view of the larger context and the lifespan of the structure. Thus a café

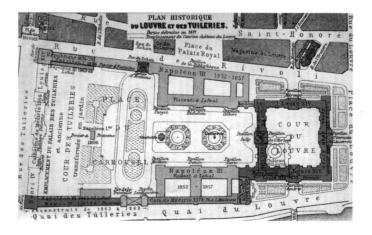

Phases of development of the Louvre Museum, from *Paris and Its Environs* by Karl Baedeker, 1913. Many built forms are transformed over time. Designers can anticipate and design for future adaptations.

Café, Istanbul. Here the most permanent levels of a building—its site and foundations—are reinhabited in a manner that retains the integrity of the urban fabric and provides a delightful surprise of a secluded below-grade café courtyard within that fabric.

on a plaza should be conceived of as an edge room of the plaza whose vitality is dependent on its connection to the life of the plaza and whose role is to support the plaza. It may do so as a café, a bookstore, or a flower market if well designed. These transformations should be easily imagined, as they share fundamental spatial characteristics of retail spaces.

We also know that things happen that we cannot fully anticipate. Nineteenth-century office building designers could not have anticipated the need for extensive computer cabling. However, if they considered that office buildings have various utilities and that these utilities might change and expand as they had previously, then they might have designed utility shafts and cable runways that could be changed and expanded. This "open" adaptation strategy allows designers to anticipate categories of change rather than specific events.

▶▶   *Anticipate the lifespan and life stages of a project, and design appropriate strategies for adaptation.*

*   *   *

With a robust knowledge of contexts and of lineages of built species, civil designers have the raw materials with which to compose. Yet there are myriad ways to use these materials. How might we add something compelling to the composition?

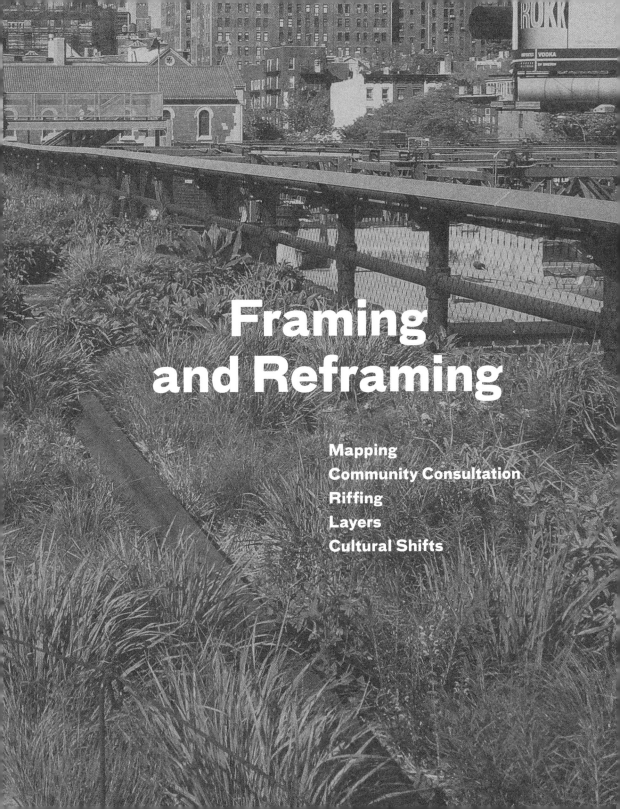

Framing
and Reframing

Mapping
Community Consultation
Riffing
Layers
Cultural Shifts

Framing and Reframing

How can deep study of context and built species become a critical tool for design? How can a designer establish *which* contexts should be major determinants of a project? For example, should the central expressions of a design be its development of regional tectonics, enrichment of an adjacent plaza, articulation of the genius loci, or some combination of these?

In civil composition, we frame critical contexts for a project. "Framing" is defining a perspective from which to evaluate the set of contexts.[1] Framing is what differentiates a classical violin from a folk fiddle. To a traffic engineer a city street may be seen as infrastructure for moving vehicles, whereas to someone trying to take a nap the street may be a source of noise, and to a shopkeeper it may be a source of customers. To a civil designer it may be all of these and more.

A project's program frames contexts. The ocean view along California's coastal highway may, for example, be fundamental for a hotel but minor for a convenience

Study of historic towers of Ouray, Colorado. The two government buildings—Walsh Library (top left) and Ouray County Courthouse (top right)—are off Main Street and have entry towers centered in symmetrical facades. The two civil society meeting places—the Beaumont Hotel (bottom right) and the Elks Lodge (bottom left)—are on the east side of Main Street and have corner towers. Each tower has a distinct upper figure seen against the backdrop of the mountains and creates distinctive rooms within the buildings.

store. Owners, bankers, regulators, neighbors, customers, contractors, and others bring their own ways of seeing to a project. The oceanside hotel may both block neighbors' views and provide customers for the convenience store. Built venues provide information about how others have framed the contexts. Perhaps the owner of an existing convenience store discovered that he can sell beach paraphernalia after opening a trail to the beach, and a new store can build on this pattern.

Designers' principles, professional responsibilities, knowledge of precedents, and the venue, tastes, and lines of inquiry condition how they evaluate contexts. These should be made as clear as possible. A designer exercising skills in prefabrication may see different opportunities than one who works with a cadre of artisans. Understanding these and other frames that come with a project illuminates the goals, values, and assumptions that stakeholders bring to creating and judging a design. A frame, if you will, sets the rules of the design game.

Within this framework of goals, designers search for rich spatial and tectonic order for the built form—a parti, or guiding scheme. A nineteenth-century member of the Académie des Beaux-Arts, Quatremère de Quincy, required his students to begin their design work by developing a parti. The parti for a house over a creek, for example, might be a box-beam covered bridge. He articulated two types of partis.

A *prendre parti* (to seize a course of action or take a stand) is a scheme that asserts its internal formal authority. This approach focuses on the project as an independent form and often downplays participation in making larger collective forms, such as the street. Prendre partis tend to emerge from building programs, tectonic study, or geometric patterning.

"*Tirer parti*," on the other hand, observes Robin Dripps, "means to take advantage of or make the best of what you find....It shifts attention away from the architectural object as an autonomous, abstract formal ideal and privileges the existing physical and political context that a design would have to engage."[2] Tirer partis are design frames distilled from existing contexts (e.g., the land, the built venue).

Both types of partis are tools to find a meaningful central organizational order for the design—a diagram that structures the project, like a sonnet or haiku pattern structures a poem. Both require design dexterity and vision. While these partis may be seen as strongly different frames, they are not truly in opposition. Indeed, a civil concinnity between a project and its contexts rests on fusing these two types of partis.

Working on only one type of parti is akin to a solo replacing a duet—the play of dialogue is missing. One simple design technique can help combine these approaches. Rather than drawing initial schemes on blank paper or computer screens, sketch over maps or photographs to create a dialogue between contexts and scheme.

Search for ways to *solve for pattern*. The poet-farmer-critic Wendell Berry coined that term to speak about solutions that solve multiple problems, satisfy a range of critical criteria, and support the health of systems.[3] Each system is embedded in others. Berry writes, "It is the nature of any organic pattern to be contained within a larger one. And so a good solution in one pattern preserves the integrity of the pattern that contains it. A good agricultural solution, for example, would not pollute or erode a watershed."[4] The aim of solving for pattern is not just to show skill but to knit together multiple goals. The adaptive reuse of New York's High Line, for example, provides a park and promenade, salvages a historic structure, draws tourists, and serves as an economic catalyst.[5]

Speaking to graduating design students, the environmentalist David Orr built on Berry's term to outline three design principles: "[First] you must see Design as a large and

The High Line by James Corner Field Operations and Diller Scofidio + Renfro, New York, 2009. The adaptive reuse of the former elevated freight railroad is a good example of solving for multiple goals.

unifying concept—quite literally the remaking of the human presence on Earth." Secondly, you need to look upstream and downstream and "cause no ugliness, human or ecological, somewhere else or at some later time." Finally, Orr urges us to frame civil design within a generation's "great work" (ours, he argues, is addressing climate change), as opposed to "expressionist form making."[6]

Projects in turn reframe their contexts. T. S. Eliot claimed of literature that "what happens when a new work of art is created is something that happens simultaneously to all the works of art that preceded it. The existing monuments form an ideal order among themselves, which is modified by the introduction of the new (the really new) work of art among them."[7] In this way, the *Fremont Troll* (1990) by Steve Badanes, Will Martin, Donna Walter, and Ross Whitehead in Seattle recasts leftover space under a bridge as home for a community landmark, and has prompted a number of responses.

Less beneficially, in the mid-1980s One Liberty Place broke the gentlemen's agreement not to exceed the height of the statue of William Penn on Philadelphia's City Hall, thereby destroying the crafted skyline and unleashing a reframing of the sense of downtown Philadelphia. The difference between the troll statue and the Philadelphia skyscraper is that the statue improved an undervalued place and added to the commonwealth; the skyscraper destroyed a shared public value.

This chapter presents tools for framing and reframing built-form contexts: mapping, community consultation, riffing, multiple frames, and making principled responses to cultural shifts.

Fremont Troll by Steve Badanes, Will Martin, Donna Walter, and Ross Whitehead, Seattle, 1990. The troll transformed the underside of a bridge into a community landmark. Responses to the troll have included the naming of a local beer, a Trolloween festival, and statues of the Three Billy Goats Gruff.

Mapping

▶   Can we use mapping to frame and reframe design propositions?

The 1748 map of Rome by the Italian architect Giambattista Nolli, *La Pianta Grande di Roma*, is claimed to be "the first accurate map of Rome since antiquity."[8] The Nolli map set a precedent for urban cartography. It has also been a significant document for urban design, not only because it is a detailed record of venerated urban form but also because it illustrates an urban design concept of the public realm. The private space of buildings is rendered black, while the public realm of piazzas, streets, gardens, and, critically, the public interiors of buildings is white, and gardens are gray. This device illuminates a vital feature of Rome: Like Escher drawings, indoor and outdoor spaces compose one another, and the public domain occupies both types of rooms.

Maps are framing tools. They are not simple recordings of facts, but rather rest on both a selection of what to map and how to represent those subjects. Civil designers can make depictions, like Nolli's map, of morphological principles, typological variations, and other concepts of composition to help understand, frame, and reframe contexts. Mapping a project's contexts requires designers to select subjects and find means to depict their spatial distribution while inviting exploration of how a project may live within these maps.

Maps are ancient tools. Paleolithic rock art from 30,000 BCE contains maplike features, and there are surviving map artifacts from 3500 BCE.[9] In the late twentieth and early twenty-first centuries, there has been an active examination of the production, definition, interpretation, and use of maps.[10] Principles from this rich discipline that can aid civil designers follow.

Naming

Choosing the title or name for a map can be a means to make explicit the conceptual frame or line of inquiry that the map is intended to explore. Civil designers should consider developing both a short and a long title. The short title is the easy-to-use handle, ideally with some poetic density. The long title articulates the line of inquiry. For example, a long title might read: *A Fabric of Brownstones: Town-form and architectural characteristics of historic buildings within the daily experience of users of the proposed design. Buildings on or*

right
Detail of *La Pianta Grande di Roma*,
map of Rome by Giambattista Nolli
(also known as the Nolli Map), 1748.
Note how the types of spaces are
indicated—private interior spaces as
black, public interior spaces as white
within walls, public exterior spaces as
white, and gardens as patterns.

below
Amsterdam map, from *Belgium and
Holland, Handbook for Travelers* by
Karl Baedeker, 1910. The blue lines of
this map draw attention to a vast
landscape of waterways, of which
Amsterdam is just a part.

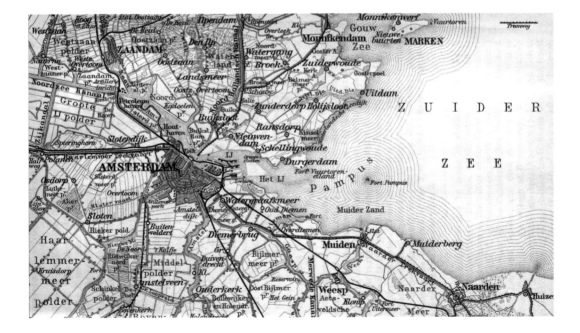

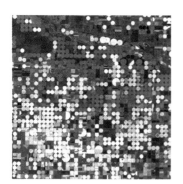

Center pivot irrigation landscape near Garden City, Kansas, from the USGS series *Earth as Art*. Each is labeled: "Satellite scene chosen for aesthetic interest rather than for scientific interpretation," underscoring the multiple frames we bring to images.

nominated to the National Historic Register within the district, indicating categories of historic significance (e.g., historic event, architectural style) and showing morphological, typological, and detail characteristics of significant styles. Writing these titles helps articulate why you are making the map and illuminates your assumptions. Why, in the above title, does the study include structures nominated to the register or limited to "the district?" For that matter, why is the register the appropriate yardstick to measure "historic buildings"? The point is to uncover your assumptions, bias, and positions in order to make maps that ground and inspire your design and may be used to discuss proposed designs with others.

The distinction between maps used for visualization versus those used for illustration is vital to civil design. The aim of visualization is to *discover* rather than to illustrate what is already known or assumed.[11] Context maps should be created to understand contexts and used as canvases on which to sketch design propositions. In a sense, civil designers should first create tools from contexts and then use these tools to craft their proposals.

Map Making

Civil designers should also create their own culture and techniques of map making. The frame of scientific inquiry often associated with map making can be useful for design, but it is not the only potential frame. Map making is also conceived as a mode of storytelling and of art production.[12] The landscape architect James Corner's diagrams of environmental and cultural emergence, the landscape architect Lawrence Halprin's urban choreography, and the landscape architect Randolph Hester's places of the heart illustrate different practices.[13] Map making as design-framing can borrow from all of these modes. As we develop this practice, we would do well to consider the following questions.

Who should make design maps? The urban planner and author Kevin Lynch's practice of asking people to draw sketch maps of places in order to construct collective mental maps, and Hester's collectively made maps of places of the heart, illustrate strengths of community-made maps.[14] In addition to using existing maps and creating your own, it may be fruitful to develop practices for asking clients, project users, and other stakeholders to make maps.

What should be mapped? The chapter "Contexts" outlines a potential set of contexts that could inform design maps. Care should be taken in gathering data for these maps.

Data sources inevitably have their own definitions and limitations. This is vitally important if the source is your own observation. Nolli's definition of public space, for example, may not have been shared across all citizens. Did women, the poor, or children have substantially equivalent access as wealthy men to the places Nolli mapped in white? Similarly, the courts and rookeries where the urban poor lived in Victorian towns were often left off maps of the era.[15]

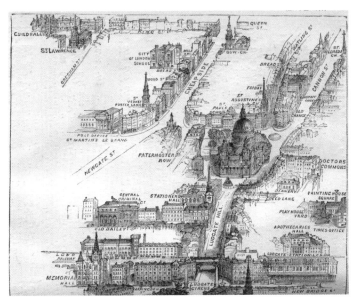

FLEET STREET AND LUDGATE HILL,
TO ST. PAUL'S AND CHEAPSIDE, &c.

Map of Fleet Street, London, illustrated by T. Sulman, from *London in 1880*, 1880. This guidebook extolled its bird's-eye views of streets, which allowed readers to grasp each scene at a glance.

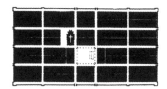

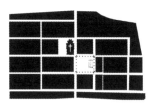

Three variations of a figure/ground diagram of the French *bastide* Monpazier. Each emphasizes different aspects of the place.
Top: An often-used diagram redrawn from *L'Architecture Française* by Marie Dormoy, 1935, showing an idealized complete plan.
Middle: A diagram using the same level of detail created from an aerial view.
Bottom: Building footprints, instead of the blocks, are shown in black.

Mapping is not limited to a snapshot in time. Corner and other landscape urbanists create evolutionary maps to describe and shape development of landscapes over time. Similarly, diagrams of building sequencing are four-dimensional design maps.

How does the point of view change the map? Plan views, bird's eyes, skylines, and transects each have their benefits and biases. We must also consider the conceptual point of view embodied in a map. Is the map intended to record a verifiable (scientific) view, a shared narrative (e.g., the narrative landscape of Route 66), personal observations (e.g., psychogeographic maps), political-social advocacy, or cultural criticism (e.g., a map of Ecotopia)?[16] How do the concepts of mistakes and lies vary according to the point of view?

What means of representation should we use? Each choice of means of production, graphic conventions, scale, views, and composition literally changes the way we see and evaluate a topic. It is often beneficial to use photography to produce base maps, as photographs capture information that we did not see at the time. Conversely, hand drawing a scene may inspire us to understand relationships that would otherwise go unexplored.

The framing power of graphic convention is illustrated by the use of figure/ground diagrams to describe and analyze a pattern of existing public spaces. Used well, these diagrams allow designers to focus between buildings and see the implied spaces. But not all spatial edges are delineated simply by solid buildings. A canopy of trees, for example, defines the park in the center of many of the squares in Savannah, Georgia. Furthermore, the three-dimensional form of similar two-dimensional spaces can significantly differ. The streets of Chicago are enclosed by buildings in a distinctly different way than those on the hills of San Francisco. There may be multiple public spaces of many different scales overlapping and nested within one another. For example, Speakers' Corner, a storied place in itself, is a portion of London's Hyde Park and an extension of the Marble Arch area. The ownership and spatial practices of spaces will not appear on figure/ground drawings. Formal gardens, for instance, will be indistinguishable from parking lots and sidewalks. However, none of these spaces should be dismissed. The least noble may have the greatest possibility for reinvention.

How do our projects remap places? As designers we not only study places, we propose their modification. Thus we should map, remap, and anticipate that remapping will continue, perhaps even preparing maps of plausible responses to our projects.

Maps as Devices

Maps embody rhetorical, economic, and political power. Zoning maps are a prime example of maps as instruments of municipal power. Even without being made as direct instruments of design, both map making conventions and maps themselves can drive physical design. Country roads, town grids, and state boundaries have been located based on the U.S. land survey, and thus, de facto, that survey is one of the most extensive acts of design on the planet.

Our design products are often maps. A set of construction documents is a map used to build a project and is thus an instrument of power. How we make our maps can alter the practices of construction trades, regulators, financial agents, lawyers, and others, and, in turn, these people shape how we make our maps.

Sometimes our designs are not construction maps but other kinds of design maps. Site studies of potential building configurations may be used to secure funding, challenge regulations, or anticipate environmental loads. Design editors (see "Design Editors") regularly use maps—such as zoning, platting, and type diagrams—to shape design venues.

▶▶ *Make multiple maps emphasizing different contexts of a site. Carefully select the subject, tools, and participants for each line of inquiry so that the map may yield new insights or agreements. Develop your designs on these maps, and make new maps as the design evolves.*

Community Consultation

▶   How can designers talk with communities to
     gain knowledge, storylines, and ideas to define
     critical frames?

Gathering information about, and evaluating all potentially
relevant contexts for, a project can be an overwhelming task.
But consulting a project's affected stakeholders and observers
can significantly aid in context framing. This community
can provide information about contexts, may represent the
tastes and desires of potential customers and users of a project,
and can represent the frames and values of neighbors and
others who have a say in approval. Consulting with communities may uncover potential design ideas, allow for community
opinions to change and develop in a way that marketing surveys
or site reconnaissance cannot, and build a sense of community
ownership, or at least acceptance, of a project. There is a
Kenyan proverb that "having a good discussion is like having
riches."

        Moreover, community dialogue can address an ethical
issue of civil composition. In many arts, an audience member
may choose without significant consequence to engage and
disengage with a work. We can buy and then put down a
book, or go to a movie and walk out. These arts have voluntary
audiences. Likewise, the owners of built places are voluntary
audiences. However, buildings, landscapes, and public
works also have significant involuntary audiences, including

A designer diagrams and talks
with students at the site of
a high school courtyard remodel.
Employing multiple methods for
consultation and adapting to
the milieu of those consulted can
improve communications.

nonowner users, neighbors, passersby, and citizens. Think of the wide variety of people who are involuntarily affected by built forms such as a confusing network of hospital corridors or a power substation that erodes the character of a beloved neighborhood. This is, of course, the basis for building and zoning codes. As professionals, civil designers are charged with both serving clients' needs and advocating for the public good. To do so may require going well beyond legal requirements.

Governments, corporations, developers, and conventional clients typically can represent their economic and programmatic interests well. The interests of stakeholders such as nonprofits, community groups, tenants, and future generations may not be as well represented; designers should work to understand these interests. Robust community dialogue can provide a venue for affected parties to have a voice.

Designers sometimes are concerned that talking with stakeholders will erode their design authority or waste their time. Both can happen. But talking with someone does not equal ceding authority to them. Understanding how design authority is already distributed for a project (see "Webs of Authorship" in "Infectious Design"), setting clear goals for consultation, and designing the format for dialogue can help make community consultation productive. Another view of the designer's community role is embodied in the Inuit saying, "The storyteller is the one who makes space for the story to be told."[17]

Clear goals for consultation help set expectations, define limits, and measure success. Consultation goals will vary according to the players and their relative authority and knowledge. Different goals for community consultation are appropriate for each of the design phases of gathering context information, framing, envisioning partis, developing designs, construction, and maintenance. Developing a maintenance agreement in which a neighboring retirement community takes care of a garden, for example, requires very different goals and tools than does consulting the local historical society to gather narratives of place. Interactions at early phases of design can provide groundwork for agreements at later phases.

There are myriad potential formats for consultation, and these too must be shaped to the instance, goals, and resources. When developing a format, consider whom to consult, what tools of discussion will be used (e.g., surveys, roundtable talks, public testimony), who will host the meeting, where and when it will take place, how long it will last, the implied and stated desired outcomes, and how others may try to reframe your format to other ends (e.g., protesting business practices at a planning board meeting, or talking at a design charrette to position themselves for public office).

INTERVIEWS, SURVEYS, AND FOCUS GROUPS: These formats are useful for gathering contextual information such as the history of the built venue, stories of place, or neighbors' conceptions of a site and district. First you should determine who has the information, how to systematically ask for it, and what you are offering implicitly or explicitly in return. For example, nonprofits, universities and scholars, and governmental agencies often have gathered and formatted information. They want it used and want credit for providing it. On the other hand, neighbors often have not organized their views and may desire information and a voice about potential designs.

PRESENTATIONS AND DISCUSSIONS: Presenting information about a project to a business association, neighborhood organization, or the friends of the park is a well-established method for eliciting contextual information, frames of view, design ideas, implied or overt consent, and occasionally collaboration. Presenting drafts of context maps, alternate schemes, and possible modes of collaboration (e.g., a community garden or a competition for local artists) can help elicit and frame responses.

COMMUNITY CHARRETTES: Hosting a design exercise and inviting a full range of stakeholders to participate is a complicated affair typically used for large projects with a complex set of interested parties. Having many of the affected parties in the room can facilitate dialogue and negotiation. Exhibiting the design process and allowing feedback can aid in obtaining consent, and the pressure of a timeline can streamline decision making. But charrettes can be difficult to organize well, and they require a degree of openness and even playfulness from all involved. There are bodies of literature on how to conduct a charrette. The National Charrette Institute, for example, is a nonprofit whose mission is to teach a charrette format through courses and publications. Likewise, the American Institute of Architects has a long history of organizing Regional/Urban Design Assistance Teams.[18] Full-blown charrettes are not appropriate for small projects, but the principles may apply on a smaller scale. Spending the day sketching with homeowner clients and inviting the neighborhood design review committee can accomplish many of the same goals.

PUBLIC HEARINGS: Governmental bodies such as a planning commission often take public comment through the public hearing format. This is typically a highly prescribed legal process in which the public is allowed to make short verbal statements to a decision-making body. Civil designers typically provide information to advocate for (or, less often, against) a project. Hearings often occur late in the process and influence parties to take strong positions. They do, however, provide a check against designers or clients who discount public interests.

In addition to the above palette of tools for dialogue, civil designers have developed a few specialized tools. Image-based discussions ask audiences to rate (and more importantly) to discuss images chosen to explore relevant design questions. There is also a vigorous practice of developing design games for community consultation. Games may ask groups to make trade-offs between programmatic pieces (e.g., a garage versus a mother-in-law cottage), arrange buildings on a site to produce public spaces, or come to a consensus and tell a story about what types of facades fit in a neighborhood. The architect Michael Pyatok uses design games to help develop housing projects.[19] Community mapping projects in which stakeholders map various aspects of a context or milieu may be particularly helpful at the initial stages of design.[20]

No matter the format, the question of who hosts a discussion is significant. Hosting your own meeting allows for inviting a broad audience and taking control of the agenda, place, and schedule. It also, however, attracts people most actively concerned (often negatively) with the project and involves more work than attending meetings of existing groups. It also may not produce the same goodwill that attending others' meetings can. In all cases, clarity of goals and respect for the participants is necessary for useful dialogue.

▶▶   *Develop multiple means to listen to and talk with stakeholders and observers. Consult with them to evaluate and frame contexts, develop schemes, refine details, and perhaps construct, furnish, or maintain the built form.*

Community Arts Learning Center

Workshop using a "room allocation game" for a proposed community arts learning center in Reidsville, North Carolina. Groups of stakeholders—council members, artists, citizens, etcetera—used the "game board" to form a consensus on the new organization of rooms in an existing building.

Riffing

▸ How can you respond to a built form, evoke
a design tradition, or "quote" a designer without
merely copying?

Riffing, a term that originates in jazz, is improvising on a
pattern. It may happen between two musicians during a piece,
or over time and in separate works. Riffing allows for a "call and
response" dialogue between artists (for one artist to refer to and
transform another's work) and for development of a tradition,
style, type, or genre. In urban composition, riffing is essential
for the creation of urban patterns such as a district or a regional
style, and allows for a dialogue of professional precedents.
The folk musician Pete Seeger quotes his father about musical
borrowing—"plagiarism is basic to all culture"—and discusses
"the folk process" of music passed from musician to musician
and altered by each.[21]

 The boundary between productive artistic borrowing and
plagiarism is a social-legal construct that itself develops over
time from interactions of multiple parties.[22] At one pole, riffing
is the shared play (or argument) of a community of artists, and
at the other extreme, true plagiarism is the sham of presenting
another's work as one's own. Different legal cultures have
developed different principles to navigate between these poles.
The European concept of artists' moral rights protects the

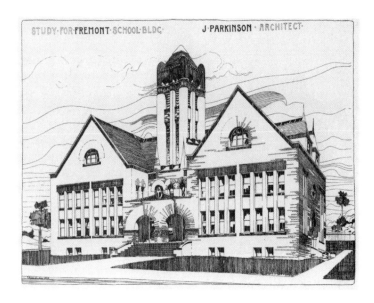

Study for the B. F. Day School
by John Parkinson, Seattle, from
*American Architect and Building
News*, November 1891. This scheme
and much of Parkinson's earlier
work was in the Richardsonian
Romanesque style. Henry Hobson
Richardson's work inspired projects
across the United States and in
other parts of the world.

personal and reputational value of a work to its author (e.g., the right to have a say about the context in which a work is displayed). The British "sweat of the brow" doctrine protects the work of compiling, for example, a telephone directory. U.S. copyright doctrine does not, but rather requires some degree of creativity.

U.S. copyright protects the fixed expression of ideas, not the ideas themselves. In U.S. legal doctrine, the more derivative rather than transformative the reuse of a design is, the more it tends toward copyright infringement. However, *scènes à faire*—aspects that are customary to a genre, such as a shootout in a Western movie or false fronts on Main Street buildings in the West—are not protected by copyright.

When determining fair use, U.S. courts will consider the normal practices of a professional community. What then should be normal practice for urban composition? First, as this book argues, urban composition is dependent on a robust practice of riffing so that individual built forms create larger forms and provide a set of collective goods. Built forms should also respond to, and add to, the professional body of practice in order to advance the professional dialogue. However, each project inhabits a unique constellation of contexts, which

Santa Caterina Market by Enric Miralles and Benedetta Tagliabue, Barcelona, 2005. The new market roof echoes Antoni Gaudí's (and others') motifs by using boldly colored tiles, sensuous curves, and elaborated roofscapes. The roof also helps compose the street and serves as an eye-catcher to draw people from the Barcelona Cathedral plaza.

means that derivative copying is poor urban composition. Yet the constraints of a niche, urban morphologies, programmatic conventions, and the history of a built species constitute *scènes à faire* that help create larger forms and practices.

Based on a set of case studies, the lawyer and architect Paul Byard proposes three categories of riffing in additions— extending the meaning of the first work (as Bernini's 1667 colonnade brings Saint Peter's Basilica into the fabric of Rome), deriving new meanings from the first work (similar to the British architect Sir Christopher Wren's integration of a royal hunting pavilion (1635) designed by the British architect Inigo Jones into the campus of the 1715 Royal Naval Hospital at Greenwich), and transforming the meaning of the old project (as Scarpa's 1964 redesign of Castelvecchio reinterpreted the fourteenth-century castle as an art museum and artwork).[23]

The scholar William Hubbard proposed another model for built-form riffing: case law, the written decisions of judges.[24] Analyzing the means by which case law both presents a coherent tradition and reflects and responds to current conditions, Hubbard developed six approaches to subsuming earlier works.

Fred and Ginger by Vlado Miluni and Frank Gehry, Prague, 1996. The design respects and transforms Prague's collection of neobaroque, neo-Gothic, and art nouveau facades, even following the established morphological pattern of placing a figural component at the corner of a block.

Fred and Ginger (the 1996 Nationale-Nederlanden building by Vlado Miluni and Frank Gehry) in Prague is an example of what Hubbard calls "swerving," or following earlier patterns up to a point and then providing a more compelling next component. "Completion"—showing that previous patterns were not comprehensive or brought to their logical conclusion—is illustrated by Florence's Piazza della Santissima Annunziata. Eighty-nine years after Brunelleschi designed an arcade on the site, the architects Antonio da Sangallo the Elder and Baccio d'Agnolo mirrored his work to complete the piazza.[25] Hubbard's "focusing"—demonstrating that the earlier work was too general—could be accomplished by remodeling a clone franchise store to articulately respond to its contexts. "Self-limitation"—picking only a few aspects of the earlier work to use in a new design—is illustrated by the Swedish architect Erik Asplund's 1937 addition to the Göteborg Law Courts in Sweden, which have modernist elevations abstracted from the existing seventeenth-century building facades.[26] Scarpa's redesign of Castelvecchio brings new meaning to an old form and thus is an example of "refilling," and Aldo Rossi's Teatro del Mondo (1979) embodies the essential gestures of earlier form, and thus "evokes the essence" of Venice.

Göteborg Law Courts addition by Erik Asplund, Sweden, 1937.

I believe that neither Byard's nor Hubbard's taxonomies can ever be complete. We continue to develop new ways to make addenda, quotes, rejoinders, and replies. The techniques outlined in "Naturalizing Clones" (in "Built Species") could be used to transform other built species. Changing niche perspective can radically reframe a project. A freeway bridge, for example, can become a bat rookery, a warehouse can become a loft, or, evoking the fictive landscape, a telephone pole can become a dragon roost.

▶▶   *Riff on existing built forms to create collective forms and practices. Transform what you borrow to articulately fit your project's contexts, support collective goods, and add to professional dialogue.*

Layers

▶ Can a design respond to different and perhaps contradictory contexts?

A mark of a great work is that it appeals to multiple audiences at the same time through collage or polyvalence. The story of blind men describing an elephant according to what part they are touching suggests one possible use of collage. Neighbors of a children's clinic, for example, are likely to be most concerned about the outside of the building—its facades, massing, parking, and such. Staff and patients may be most focused on the inside. Bold architectural publicity photographs may show views that are not central to either group's concerns. A designer could appeal to each audience in the areas it touches and meet his or her own standards for coherence through artful collage of the parts.

Finding the views that different stakeholders value may enrich the design by introducing a degree of complexity and contradiction. Responding to these different views could yield a dynamic parti: a children's clinic might have a subdued outer shell responding to neighbors' desires that encloses a playful

24 Peck Slip by Cook+Fox Architects, New York, 2006. This building's Front Street and Peck Slip facades respond to and help create streets with significantly different characters while maintaining an integrated building design.

and private courtyard to serve the children. Likewise, the great nineteenth- and twentieth-century European urban railroad termini wrapped industrial sheds with urban *hôtels* to unify the disparate contexts of railroad and city.

Because different audiences bring to bear different values and knowledge, they can see different aspects of a project, allowing for polyvalent readings. Shakespeare could write to many audiences at once. His dirty jokes and swordplay appealed to the cheap seats, while his plot twists entertained those focused on the storyline, and his existential questions rewarded long contemplation. His works are of his time, yet reach back to older stories and have inspired later generations. A great built form can evoke a diverse set of readings, too. It may provide a contemporary brandable image while also complementing a historic district, operating carbon neutrally, comfortably displaying a delight in state-of-the-art engineering and use of artisanal materials, and responding to the other-worldliness of a local winter ice fog and the scruffiness of the back alley.

Every built element holds potential for multiple meanings. Bridges, for example, both connect two banks and make manifest their separation. They may be seen as of the land, the river, and the sky. They are fixed objects that embody movement, and passages that provide unique places for standing still.[27] Evoking multiple meanings allows different audiences to read different stories and for audiences to reread a story in new ways.

Layers can also respond to different scales of context. The siting and structure of a building on a window-shopping street, for example, should establish the structure as a room off the sidewalk. The facade, signage, window displays, and aromas can declare that it is currently a bakery.

A strong collage of layers will explore conflicts, commonalities, and scales of context. One can root for the   Red Sox, the Yankees, and the game all from the same stadium.

▶▶ *Find means such as collage and polyvalence to allow multiple readings of a built form but also to create a larger frame that explores the conflicts and commonalities of the views in which the perspectives operate.*

Cultural Shifts

▶   How can civil designers best participate
    in cultural reframings?

The larger culture, of course, frames and reframes the built
environment. Telluride, Colorado, was built as a mining
town, which dwindled as the mines played out. Then, in the
1970s, it was reconceived as a ski town and cultural nexus.
Civil designers were involved, but the transformation was a
larger political-cultural-economic struggle. Likewise, the rise
of Chicago as a skyscraper city certainly involved designers but
was driven by a technological-economic-cultural shift.[28]

Wigwam burner, Cascade
mountains, Washington. In the
twentieth century, many lumber
mills burned sawdust and other
"waste" wood in metal structures
like this. These distinct towers
were iconic markers of lumber
towns. Due to shifts in technology,
economics, and regulations, these
structures are no longer built
and rarely used.

Design of a gas and service station
by Malcolm P. Cameron, from
American City Magazine, May 1928.
Cameron's second-prize-winning
design was for a competition
sponsored by Mrs. John D.
Rockefeller, the American Civic
Association, and the Art Center of
New York. Design competitions can
help shape an emerging type.

Civil designers participate in these cultural shifts both by developing built forms that respond to, support, and embody transformations, and by participating in cultural dialogue (see "Public Professionals" in "Design Editors"). John Habraken points out that "with Palladio, who, in service to a new class of patron, reinvented the farmhouse villa…the idea of inventing new typologies took root."[29] During the rise of the automobile, civil designers and engineers actively helped develop residential and commercial garages, gas stations, traffic signals, drive-ins, drive-throughs, motels, parking lots, freeways, automobile suburbs, and numerous other built species.[30] The concurrent, century-long rise of electrical transmission and telecommunications continues to engender profound changes in built form, such as the medical teleconsultation suite and the ATM lobby.[31]

How can civil designers best participate in these cultura! reframings? This is a question of professional ethics. I suggest that we should neither simply follow the crowd—deflecting responsibility to the market or the zeitgeist—nor complain from the sidelines. In many ways, a civil designer's job is the same for any project: Ask how the design supports the public trust. Can we develop projects and shape built species that steward the environment, safeguard and encourage public health and safety, foster civil society, and help fashion creative milieus? At times, this may be a kind of quiet insurgency, perhaps offering more environmentally responsible aspects than a client asked for and justifying them in economic or other terms, or designing large vacation homes so that they can easily be converted to multifamily compounds. At other times, it may be declining or negotiating the goals of a commission. Publishing your design principles, signing onto a group's mission (e.g., the 2030 Challenge), and helping to develop professional standards of practice can aid in negotiating and working with clients and other parties in reframing design goals.

Uncovering small cultural shifts and proposing new built forms (or, more often, modifications to existing built species) is an ongoing role of civil designers. Activities that regularly occur despite the built form are indications that a built form has not adapted to shifts in cultural practices. When a new place is built to adapt to these practices, a new (sub)species is emerging. The Fremont Outdoor Cinema in Seattle is one example of an emerging built-form type.

The added challenge during cultural shifts is that precedents need to be reframed to fit substantially new

Outdoor concert at a grocery store parking lot, Hatch, New Mexico. The design of new grocery store parking lots in the Southwest and Mexico should accommodate this emerging practice.

Fremont Outdoor Cinema, Seattle. After the cinema was displaced from its original site, this second incarnation incorporates key features such as a western screen wall (to produce a dark screen at twilight), enclosure on multiple sides, a projection booth, and signage for both the cinema and parking.

Street in Cuzco, Peru, showing a marked cultural shift with Spanish-era plastered walls built atop Inca-era stone walls.

conditions. The automobile garage borrowed from the horse stable, but with significant differences.[32] The British prison, hospital, asylum, and workhouse descended from the disaggregation of the pre-1834 British poorhouse.[33] All the tools in this chapter can aid in proposing reframings, but ultimately society as a whole will test the value of individual proposals and emerging built species.

Many argue that the most important cultural shift of the twenty-first century is managing carbon use in a world with declining cheap oil, escalating climate change, and a need to reduce greenhouse gases. Built-form design and urban patterns can certainly reduce energy use and transportation demand. More subtly, we are starting to see a relocalization of culture based on things (e.g., local foods and materials) but a continued globalization of ideas (e.g., music, telemedicine). Design for resilience is insurance against the effects of climate change. Home gardens, root cellars, water cisterns, bicycle facilities, and other local, low-power systems provide a buffer against disruptions.

Other emerging shifts may shape the built environment in the years to come (e.g., machine intelligence, responsive environments, and the aging population). Major changes often emerge from quiet beginnings. Careful attention to contexts may provide civil designers with early insights.

▶▶   *Help shape cultural shifts by designing reframed and new project types that support the collective goods of civil composition.*

* * *

Designing a stance within and about a set of contexts, combining prendre and tirer partis, is an essential act of urban composition. Its quality is measured by the degree to which it provides and improves collective goods. It should also inspire subsequent designs to continue supporting these collective goods.

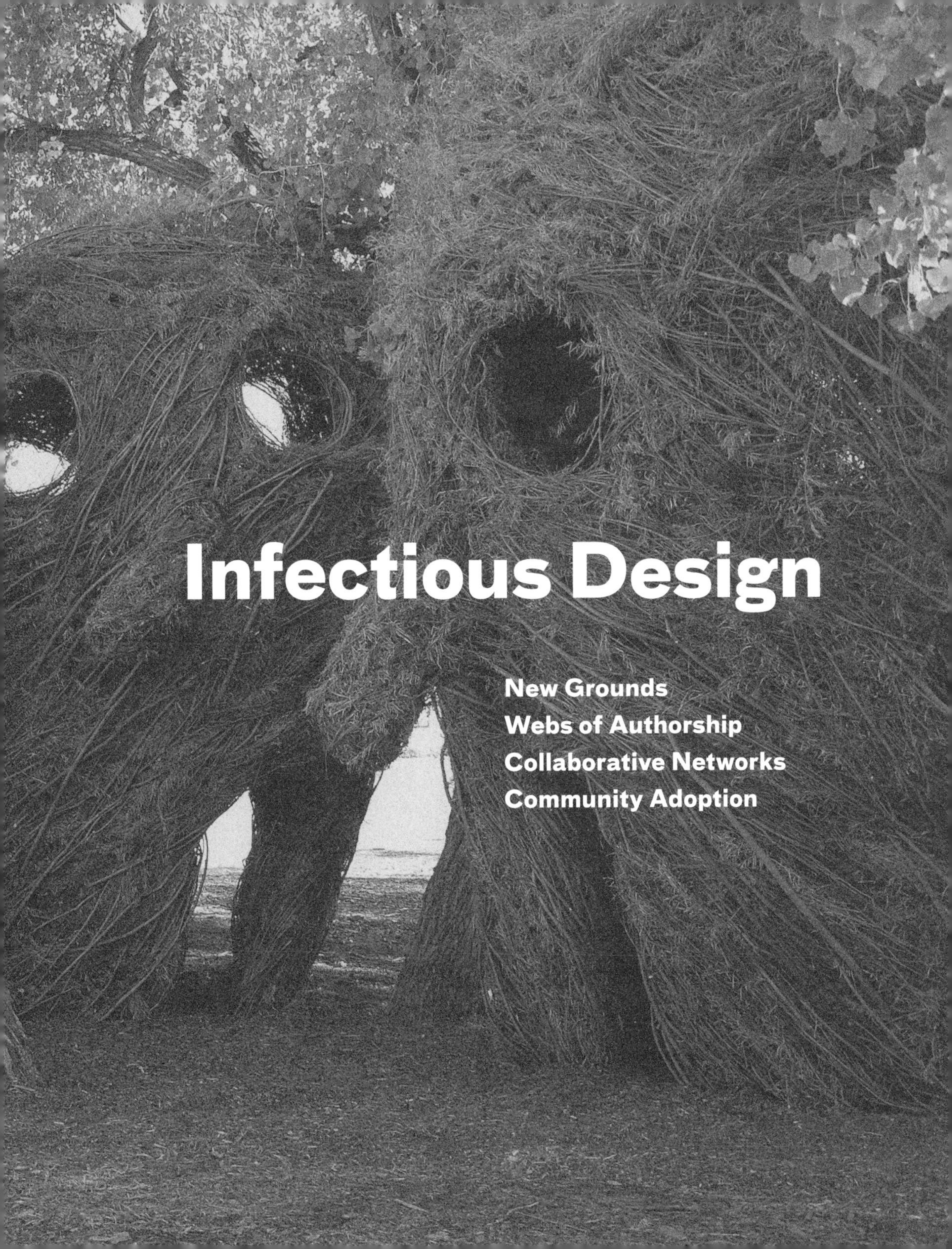

Infectious Design

New Grounds
Webs of Authorship
Collaborative Networks
Community Adoption

Infectious Design

> You think that because you understand "one" that you
> must therefore understand "two" because one and one make
> two. But you forget that you must also understand "and."
> —Sufi teaching story [1]

How might a built form inspire others to add to the collective
goods of a composition?

The principle of the second man, according to the
urban designer and architect Edmund Bacon, is that "the
second man … determines whether the creation of the first
man will be carried forward or destroyed." [2] In the economic
sense, this principle was true of new railroad towns across
the West. Many attracted settlers, and the town grid filled
in and expanded. Other towns failed. It is also true in the
compositional sense. The authors Kathy Edwards and Esmé
Howard describe the mutually reinforcing combination of
street design, program of monuments, and houses for the
wealthy that created and expanded Monument Avenue in
Richmond, Virginia. [3]

To create synergy, the response of the second designer
need not be affable. For example, the great Italian architect
and artist Francesco Borromini designed the church of Saint
Agnese in Rome. His rival Gian Lorenzo Bernini was the
sculptor of the fountain of the Four Rivers (1651) in front of
the church. In a likely apocryphal story, Bernini said that one
of the figures in his composition has his hands up to shield
his eyes from the facade of Saint Agnese. [4] Similarly, Las Vegas
can be seen as the site of a surreal boasting contest with each
new casino attempting to outdazzle those before it.

below, left
Downtown Artesia, New Mexico,
ca. 1902. With just a few buildings and
a windmill, the founders of Artesia
sketched out Main Street and implied
a future grid of cross-streets. The
founders shared a set of concepts
about the form of the future street,
and they built up to the line of the
future sidewalk to create a collective
form.

below, right
Statue in the Fountain of the Four
Rivers, Rome, by Bernini, "shielding
itself from the sight of" the church of
Saint Agnese by Borromini.

Responses, of course, need not be simple continuations of a pattern but can be transformative. Venice's Piazza San Marco emerged from a centuries-long dialogue between buildings and public space. Its current form could not have been readily predicted from its origins.[5] Responses could also show how previous work failed to achieve a public goal. For example, a remodel of a shopping mall's parking could seek to make it more sustainable, supportive of pedestrians and transit, and integrated into a neighborhood.

The economics term *virtuous cycle* describes a situation in which a series of sound economic policies sets off a chain of events in which better economic performance produces stronger currencies or other financial improvements. This in turn helps to boost economic performance further.[6]

I borrow the economic concept to describe a chain of inspiration between civil designers, and between civil designers and authors in other fields, such as fiction and painting. For instance, the Caldecott Medal–winning *Make Way for Ducklings* by Robert McCloskey is a children's story set in Boston's Public Garden. The book became so beloved that in 1987 the city of Boston installed a statue of the ducklings in the Public Garden. This is a small closed loop of a virtuous cycle—the Public Garden served as a setting for the book, the book inspired the statue, and the statue adds to the design of the garden.

I see what you mean (also known as the *Blue Bear*) by Lawrence Argent, Denver, 2005. The artwork plays with the Colorado Convention Center, its use as a meeting place, regional practices of animal iconography and chain saw art, and Denver's image as both an urban center and part of the rustic mountainous American West.

Beyond books, other examples abound. Western United States frontier towns were built with false fronts to emulate the Eastern image of a city; now the form is emblematic of the Western frontier.[7] The paintings of Taos Society of Artists from the turn of the twentieth century established Taos as an art colony and continue to influence tourism, art, and architecture. The triumphal parade affected the urban form of Rome during the Republic.[8] Peter Hall has attempted the larger project of describing the political, economic, urban, and creative cycles that lead to cities' "golden ages."[9]

Not all cycles are beneficial. The virtuous cycle of borrowing, play, and engaged argument between place and text can spin out of control and become a vicious cycle. For example, historic district regulations like those in Santa Fe, or Denver's Larimer Square, can be seen as using a master narrative to gloss over critical aspects of the past and/ or suppress the development of contemporary stories and styles. Staged cycles, such as themed shopping centers or Leavenworth, Washington, where many buildings and staff are dressed in "Bavarian style," may have some economic success. However, these affected themes displace and devalue the opportunity for cycles that embody the genius loci.

Virtuous cycles can become complex, enduring patterns of reinforcement that produce a coevolution of multiple built species and define a cultural landscape. For example, the streetcar coevolved with department stores, amusement parks, district electrical systems, and streetcar suburbs.[10]

How might we design to inspire the "second man" to respond and start a virtuous cycle? Previous chapters outlined one fundamental strategy—build upon previous work, a larger form, or other context. If you ignore or debase the built-up body of earlier work, how can you ask others to follow your work? If you show value and delight in rich contextualism, the work makes its own argument. Additionally, anticipating the life stages of a built form can help future designs follow readily from the initial work.

This chapter presents further strategies for inspiring future designers to add to a civil composition: building new ground, distributing authorship, joining groups of peers, and engaging the community.

New Grounds

▶   How can built forms create excellent sites for smaller projects within and enrich the larger compositions in which they sit?

Civil designers regularly create "new ground" for other designers—sites, contexts, rules, and precedents. Designers of one domain frequently set up conditions for designers of smaller domains. Urban planners set the context and rules for civil engineers' design of roads and drainage systems, and the architects of building shells make spaces and conditions for tenant improvements. Projects may also support larger forms. For example, the skyscrapers around Chicago's Grant Park help define the character and enclosure of this grand urban space. Creating contexts for other designers can also be conceptual, as when we establish regulatory precedents or new policies.

There are a number of practices that can help to fair-mindedly examine a project from the point of view of future designers and the niche gestalt of future projects:

First, it is important to sketch a variety of potential responses to a project, including both designs that would live

The balconies on these buildings in New Orleans are a separate design level from the main structural system. They can be repaired, replaced, or removed with minimal effect on the mass walls.

within the project (e.g., a coffee shop in your retail space) and larger forms that may emerge from the interplay of the project and others (e.g., the skyline of a town). The classic exercise of laying out two alternative furniture arrangements for rooms is an example. Sketches can test whether existing examples of the potential future designs work well with a project. For example, if a project leaves space for a courtyard, are there existing great courtyard designs that fit the space? A more rigorous approach is to have others test a design.

A second approach is consultation with civil designers who are experts in the future project type. Plaza designers, for instance, could ask a group of public artists about creating great sites for art, and likewise architects who place a building so as to imply a future square should consult with plaza designers. Designers and consultants should discuss both grand ideas and details.

Third, subsequent designs should be evaluated in multiple contexts, not just that of the project. The character and relationship to the street, for example, is often more critical to storefront retail spaces than their relationship to the skyscraper that houses them.

Finally, carefully consider which parts of a site should be durable and which readily adaptable. When new tenants take over, what will they desire to change and what assets will they wish to retain? What components need to remain stable for the larger forms?

Flatiron building, Ballard, Washington. The building creates an asset out of what might be considered a difficult, small, triangular site.

Our projects may also be a portion of a larger new ground. For example, in *A New Theory for Urban Design,* the architecture professor Christopher Alexander proposes: "Every building must create coherent and well-shaped public space next to it."[11] Likewise, new commuter rail stops create the opportunity for transit-oriented villages around these stations. Subsequent designers can respond to and build these larger forms.

This new ground may also be the extension of an existing form. Perhaps a subdivision connects an existing street through its site to the waterfront or a park. This extension redefines the character of the existing street. On occasion, we can create new ground by conceiving of projects that occupy places not previously considered sites. Designers and place artists have done this by building miniature "cliff dwellings" within eroded brick walls, turning empty lots into community gardens, redesigning a railway into a linear park, and transforming underused warehouses into apartment lofts.

We can blaze a trail by transforming rules. Powerful civil composition can convince authorities that the rules for all similar future work should be modified or recast. Replacing setbacks with build-to lines, for example, can revitalize sidewalks.

Of course, there are many subtleties to the relationships between projects. As flat-iron buildings attest, there can be great design power in resolving "irregular" and "difficult" sites. Creating excellent sites for projects is not simply leaving space for them, but rather providing conditions that set up compelling possibilities.

On the flip side of this relationship, civil designers should develop articulate means to provide feedback to designers of the sites and rules in which they operate. Designers of parades should, for instance, publish and testify about how street design standards support, impede, or ignore parades; stream restorers must help urban designers understand how to manage runoff; and civil designers of all stripes should offer their knowledge to rule makers.

▶▶ *Every design should create excellent sites for smaller projects within it and enrich larger patterns in which it sits. Test alternative options, consult with experts, consider the full range of contexts, design appropriately durable and adaptable parts, and create a field of compelling possibilities. Provide articulate feedback to the designers of sites within which you work.*

Here's Looking at You by Patrick Dougherty and students at Bosque School, Albuquerque, 2009.
A clump of trees is transformed by temporary sculptures that are also inhabitable "rooms."

Webs of Authorship

▶   How can you involve and inspire multiple designers?

Virtually all civil design projects have distributed authorship. Clients and regulators exercise various degrees of control. Regulators, in turn, frequently give authority to neighbors and other stakeholders. The tastes and habits of potential customers, buyers, and other users are often surveyed and given design weight by clients. Design firms often have teams working on a project. Outside designers, from the industrial designers of streetlights to commissioned artists, contribute parts.

Often this web of authorship is productive and allows for a diversity of information, skills, viewpoints, and goals. New ideas can emerge from interactions of multiple designers, and designs can be refined to meet multiple goals.

However, teamwork is a learned skill. Factors that help make teams work include clarity about roles, authority, and expectations; ability to remain open and even playful about ideas and options rather than taking positions; willingness to give credit to others; and frequent clear communication.[12]

Twelfth-century portion of Tossa de Mar, Spain. The form of the vine-covered restaurant in the foreground, the street, and the district arose from the actions of multiple designers over the course of generations.

Souk in Damascus, Syria, 2009.
Despite revolutionary changes
in technology, economics, and other
larger systems, this ancient place
maintains a social, economic, and
formal cohesion.

As Paul Goldberger writes of designers cooperating to
make the forms of buildings along a street, "Like dancers,
architects follow one another's lead and endeavor not to
step on any toes." [13]

The Institute of Design at Stanford University advocates
what it calls "radical collaboration"—collective work across
distinctly different disciplines. Perhaps photojournalists
could help research social practices and stories of place
for a planning department or a developer; an architectural
firm could hire an industrial designer to explore tectonic
markets; community health clinic designers could work with
master gardener associations to create health gardens; or
an environmental foundation could benefit from hiring an
architecture professor.

Too often, civil composition suffers from inadequate
distribution of authorship. In the current economy, a significant portion of development occurs in large-scale projects.
These large projects do not naturally allow for a dialogue
among independent built forms and the emergence of cultural
landscapes. Moreover, they can contribute to creating a
political or economic hegemony. This is primarily a problem of
the political economy and is beyond the control of designers of
individual projects. However, there are some design practices
that can mitigate the problems of large "single-hand" projects.

One response to this economic juggernaut is for
designers to lend intellectual, narrative, and professional
weight to smaller-scale, nonprofit, and "everyday" developers—
to what Jane Jacobs calls "gradual money." [14] Designers can

Little Italy, San Diego. The Little Italy Neighborhood Developers—a joint venture of designers and developers—divided what would have been a single block-size development into six projects that work together but are distinctly individual structures, thus perpetuating the scale and character of the neighborhood.

illustrate how large projects can be broken into phases, tenant improvements, and other components so that parts can be funded separately and involve varied designers, and so each project can provide lessons for the next. Consulting with nonprofits may inject new storylines and opportunities that a project would not otherwise have. Perhaps a low-income advocacy group has access to funding, or movie buffs could use a wall along a parking lot for outdoor movie nights. Historic preservation nonprofits can help a site retain earlier stories and enrich otherwise monothematic developments.

Another approach is to form teams of multiple developers and designers. The Little Italy Neighborhood Development in San Diego, for example, was a joint venture of designers and developers who put together a comprehensive proposal that divided a city block into six projects that work together but are distinctly individual, varying in size and character. In a *San Diego Union Tribune* article, Ann Jarmusch writes, "Architecturally, the block's collection of buildings is thrilling in concept and detail—a stimulating conversation among 'friends' who share fundamental values and vocabulary but push limits to differing degrees." [15]

Finally, overly large developments can be enriched by consulting with the community (see "Community Consultation" in "Framing and Reframing"), handing off as much design authority as possible to subsequent designers and users (as discussed in the previous section), and designing for adaptability (see "Life Stages" in "Built Species").

▶▶   *Understand and help redesign a project's web of*
      authorship to involve and inspire multiple participants
      and foster virtuous cycles of design.

Collaborative Networks

▶   How can groups of peers organize to inspire each
     other?

Logo and photograph from the Rice
Design Alliance (RDA) charrette for
Galveston, Texas. Architecture tours
and design competitions are some
of the other activities of the nonprofit
organization, whose role is to advance
the built environment in the Houston
region. RDA's diverse membership
includes architects, designers,
developers, community activists,
and others.

Formal and informal groups of peers are prime sources
for shared inspiration. Circles of colleagues, professional
organizations, community organizations, design movements,
and other collaborative networks gather to improve practice.
They aim to improve cultural landscapes, share knowledge and
aspirations, present the merits of a discipline or movement,
shape practices and standards, and develop public policy.
Some groups, such as the Friends of Pike Place Market in
Seattle, are place-based; others, such as the American Society
of Landscape Architects or Congress for the New Urbanism,
are focused on a profession or movement.

Professional groups, in particular, are responsible for the
health and collective goods of their fields. The sociologist of
professions Eliot Freidson argues that "the professional model
is based on the democratic notion that people are capable
of controlling themselves by cooperative, collective means and
that, in the case of complex work, those who perform it are in
the best position to make sure it gets done well." Such a model
provides a viable alternative to governmental or corporate
bureaucratic control or unfettered free markets, according
to Freidson.[16] These groups of "civil stewards"—accrediting
and professional organizations, educational leaders, design
columnists, etcetera—evaluate and guide the works, goals, and
practices of the professions. Following are some ways these
groups can organize to catalyze inspiration.

Comradeship—knowing that others share your
professional interests, discoveries, and difficulties—not
only is a benefit in itself but also is the ground for responding
to one another's work and for joint authorship of civil
compositions. Socializing in collaborative networks helps
build what sociologists call "social capital"—good will,
fellowship, sympathy, and personal investment in a group
of similar people.[17] The political scientist Robert Putnam
makes a distinction between "bonding" and "bridging" social
capital. A bonding group, such as a gang or clique, focuses on
distinction from others. Bridging clubs focus on an activity
or subject to provide a bridge between a mix of people.[18] For
example, a venue for landscape architects, architects, civil
engineers, planners, artists, and others interested in improving
the collective design of a city might result in more creative

collaborations than a monodisciplinary club dedicated to defending its turf.

Creating multiple methods of critiquing one another's work can foster a "culture-debating" society. In addition to looking to professional awards and magazines, groups of designers can follow the lead of writer's circles and present their work to one another for discussion. With a solid base of collegiality, these "critique circles" allow a wide and nuanced exploration of members' work. In a similar (but perhaps more ego-threatening) method, universities can sponsor "reverse critiques" in which both young and seasoned professionals present their work to a jury of students.

Groups can be formed to conduct joint education or research. Medical schools host journal clubs in which faculty, students, and professionals read and present articles to one another as a way of keeping current with a wide spectrum of professional knowledge. The League of Women Voters conducts literature reviews and local research to develop white papers on local public issues. Both of these practices could be adapted by civil designers.

Conventions and lecture series are formalized means for concentrating, vetting, sharing, recording, and perpetuating practices and knowledge. Hosts of these events should balance bonding and bridging activities, seek to maximize exchange of ideas and substantive opportunities for collaboration, and otherwise steward the professions.

Articulating collective goods, developing standards of practice, and publishing missions provide formal mechanisms to coordinate aspects of a group's work. In professional groups, these are strengthened by systems for disciplinary action. These mechanisms are the basis for professional self-governance. If they are weak or disconnected from the larger society, governments may step in to provide regulation.

Infectious design rests on not only the cogency of the work but also the environment in which it is done. Participating in and fostering multiple collaborative networks with a host of different practices can increase civil concinnity.

▶▶ *Become a steward of the profession. Join and organize groups of peers to critique one another's work, research contexts and precedents, share information and practices, establish standards and goals, and inspire others.*

Community Adoption

▶   How can designers inspire community members to "adopt" a built form?

Ultimately designers hand off their creations to users and community members. Sometimes people treat built form as an immutable given, an unchangeable landscape. In other instances, people readily play with and change built forms. This difference is partially due to social practices associated with design domains. It is typically acceptable to move an office chair or perhaps replace it with a different chair but nearly unthinkable that an employee would change the type of glass in an office window. However, built forms themselves can invite or discourage user modification.

Community members building a public space with the nonprofit Pomegranate Center, Salishan, Washington, 2008. Involving community members in design and construction of a project helps create social capital as well as ownership of the project.

Adjustable and movable parts—such as operable windows, Dutch doors, awnings, and removable bollards—provide an immediate level of adaptability that invites alteration. If windows in an office were made to readily accept user-chosen panes, they would suggest an alternative to usual social practices. Built forms may be interactive in other ways. The mirrored surface of sculptor Anish Kapoor's *Cloud Gate* (2006) in Chicago invites fun-house mirror play and photographs. Emerging electronics offers possibilities such as MIT's interactive bus stop.[19]

Hooks give permission to attach things. In rental housing, renters may not install hooks for fear of losing their deposit but would readily use them if provided. Brackets for banners on lampposts, bicycle racks on parking meters, and other connectors make attaching physically and, perhaps more significantly, socially easier.

Hooks may be broadly conceived. For example, organizational and social hooks may be provided by marking places for everything from market stalls to street performers to street posters to kickball and other games. Hooks may also be purely social practice. A public artist who would like the public to dress a statue, for example, may invite a few groups to do the first installations.

Allowing for user modification of a built place can go significantly beyond prescribed interactions. The architect Simon Nicholson developed the theory of loose parts for children's playgrounds. Nicholson suggested that playgrounds with sand, water, and other loose materials, instead of only

below, left
EyeStop by SENSEable City Laboratory, MIT (Giovanni de Niederhausern, Shaocong Zhou, Assaf Biderman, and Carlo Ratti) in collaboration with the Province of Florence and the local public transportation authority ATAF.

below, right
Waiting for the Interurban by Richard Beyer, Seattle, 1979. The work has become the site of regular "art attacks," with people dressing the project for various celebrations.

equipment with implied modes of "proper" play, allow children to design their play and inspire creativity.[20] Extending and generalizing this idea to other environments suggests pushing as many design decisions toward the user as possible. The European practice of demountable kitchens, for example, provides more user adaptability than the American practice of built-in cabinets.

At a more conceptual level, designers should evaluate how tightly scripted their designs should be. A grid of streets, for example, allows pedestrians to choose their routes, whereas a hierarchy of cul-de-sacs, collectors, and arterials makes that decision for them. Likewise, a colonnade of street trees of the same age and species may overdictate form, spread tree diseases, and look awkward if a single tree dies. Perhaps regular spacing and trees of similar habit could provide coherence yet still allow a variety of species.

Scripts and stories can enable play rather than overly control it, if they allow multiple roles and interpretations. For instance, rather than enumerating and mandating the details of a local style, a design code could act as an open script that articulates and reviews generative factors, such as material technologies, climate buffering responses, and aesthetic principles.

Finally, adopt-a-park and similar programs organize community maintenance. These programs rest on designs in which at least a portion of upkeep can be done by relatively unskilled labor. Ideally the specific type of maintenance not only provides upkeep but also is a visible investment by the community in the facility and thus deters abuses. School cleanups, for example, are intended to influence students not to litter.

▶▶ *Consider how to hand over the life of a built form to its users. Provide adjustability, hooks, stages, open storylines, and appropriate levels of maintainability.*

Design Editors

Design Editors

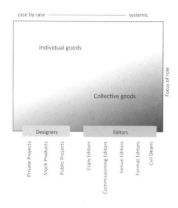

Chart of spectrum of civil composition roles, revised from Mark C. Childs, "A Spectrum of Urban Design Roles," *Journal of Urban Design* 15, no. 1 (2010).

Editor comes from the Latin *ēdere,* meaning "to put forward," and we currently use the term for work in multiple media, from print to film. Thus *editor* has broad roots that may support a reexpansion of its meaning. I propose the term *design editors* for people who help compose settlements by developing methods for individual parts to collectively achieve common goals. They are stewards of settlements. Editors of text and editors of settlements share the task of reviewing and revising the work of others. Editors collect and curate works, coach authors (of texts or designs), commission contributions, articulate visions and venues for work, and defend an open, moral dialogue. Editors in both realms aim to skillfully fit together parts to craft a whole, a concinnity of the works of multiple authors.

The focus of this book is on design author roles, but just as a writer works with editors and responds to critics and mentors, civil designers must develop fruitful ways to work with design editors. Moreover, authors become editors, and professionals serve in multiple capacities.

There are a variety of editing roles.[1] "Copy editors" review designs for their fit within larger systems, such as compliance with regulations (code official), adherence to a firm's standards (supervising designer), or fit with urban goals (design reviewer, town architect).

"Commissioning editors" research venues and cultivate design authors and projects. They may be hiring agents for a developer; crafters of competitions; or promoters of design approaches, built species, and urban patterns, as are the New Urbanists and landscape urbanists. All of these activities frame the ultimate designs and their relationships to other projects.

"Curating editors" document and develop methods to "care for the soul" of an existing district. Much urban curatorial work has come from historic preservation efforts. The architects Knud Larsen and Amund Sinding-Larsen's 2001 book *The Lhasa Atlas: Traditional Tibetan Architecture and Townscape* is a strong example of documenting a cultural landscape to set the stage for protecting it. Management of historic districts, programs to help owners rehabilitate built forms, and education programs about local design traditions are curatorial.

"Venue editors" develop a strategy for a place— design goals, venue type, tools, management structure, and vision—to shape the interactions of multiple designers in

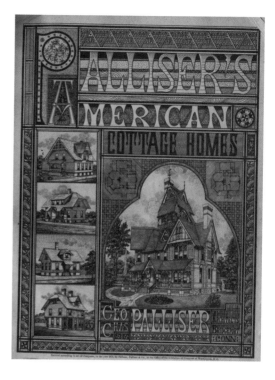

right
Cover plate from *Palliser's American Cottage Homes*, 1878. This pattern book, like Sears's later Honor Bilt kit homes and others, is the work of commissioning designers/editors who published designs to guide the development and construction of buildings.

below, left
Pattern book plate for a row house.

below, right
Pattern book plate for a three-story house.

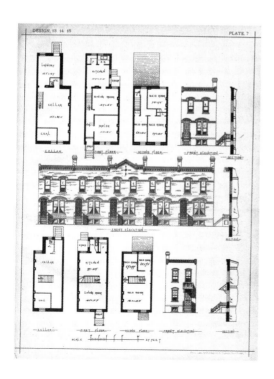

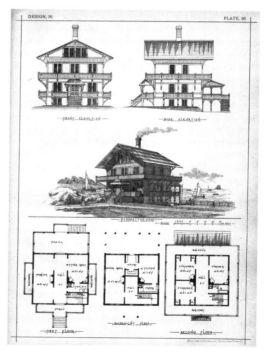

Thomas C. Hubka's analysis of the New England farm building pattern—Big House, Little House, Back House, Barn. This is an example of curatorial work. Such an analysis can illuminate adaptation to the environment and cultural patterns, curate remaining examples, and inspire new built patterns in the region.
A. Distribution and density of the pattern.
B. Development of the Woodsum Farm, illustrating incremental development.
C. Diagram of the four-field farming system associated with the building pattern.
D. Diagram of the building pattern.

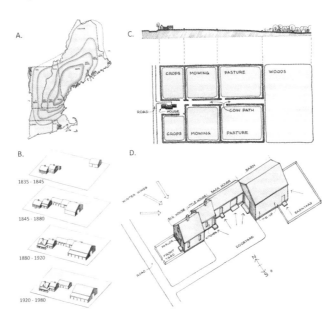

opposite
River North District, San Antonio, regulating plan and matrix of building types by Moule & Polyzoides Architects and Urbanists. This is an example of the work of a venue editor. These diagrams show types/forms of buildings allowed in each zone. Although regulating plans require more design conformity than some developments, they allow more variety within that order than the typical tract home development, and they are more considered than many developments with restrictive design covenants.

its physical (re)design. Venue editors may be comprehensive planners, subdivision designers, framers of historic or other districts, redevelopment agents, or infrastructure composers. Developers, mayors, campus architects, and urban designers are often venue editors.

"Format editors" create tools to coordinate individual projects so as to achieve collective goods. Creating the tool called "historic districts" is the work of a format editor. The tool is then available for a venue editor to create a specific historic district and hire a curator to oversee it. Examples of such tools are the New Urbanists' development of transect and form-based codes and the National Main Street Center's four-point Main Street program.

"Civil deans"—in the sense of respected professional leaders, catalysts, and advocates—evaluate and steward the goals, roles, and practices of the professions and disciplines of civil design. Palladio, Habraken suggests, set the role for modern architects and thus was the first dean of the modern era of architecture.[2] New York's "master builder" Robert Moses certainly defined an infrastructural urban design role, and Frederick Law Olmsted was a dean of modern American landscape architecture.

Additionally, every great author is also a strong self-editor and editor of context, downplaying some aspects and reinforcing or reinterpreting others.

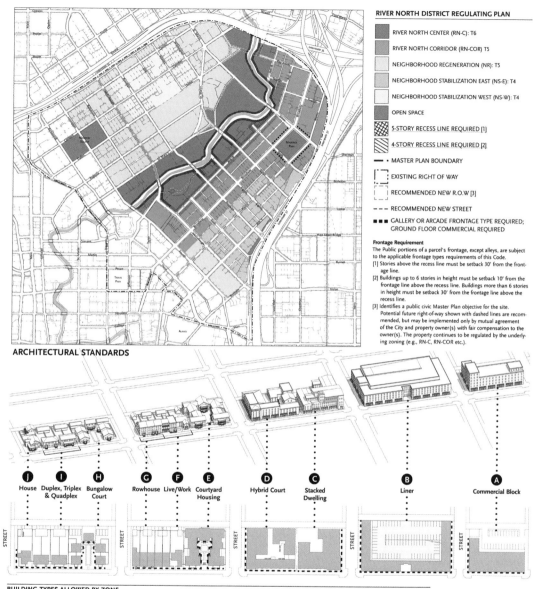

RIVER NORTH DISTRICT REGULATING PLAN

- RIVER NORTH CENTER (RN-C): T6
- RIVER NORTH CORRIDOR (RN-COR) T5
- NEIGHBORHOOD REGENERATION (NR): T5
- NEIGHBORHOOD STABILIZATION EAST (NS-E): T4
- NEIGHBORHOOD STABILIZATION WEST (NS-W): T4
- OPEN SPACE
- 5-STORY RECESS LINE REQUIRED [1]
- 4-STORY RECESS LINE REQUIRED [2]
- MASTER PLAN BOUNDARY
- EXISTING RIGHT OF WAY
- RECOMMENDED NEW R.O.W [3]
- RECOMMENDED NEW STREET
- GALLERY OR ARCADE FRONTAGE TYPE REQUIRED; GROUND FLOOR COMMERCIAL REQUIRED

Frontage Requirement

The Public portions of a parcel's frontage, except alleys, are subject to the applicable frontage types requirements of this Code.

[1] Stories above the recess line must be setback 30' from the frontage line.

[2] Buildings up to 6 stories in height must be setback 10' from the frontage line above the recess line. Buildings more than 6 stories in height must be setback 30' from the frontage line above the recess line.

[3] Identifies a public civic Master Plan objective for the site. Potential future right-of-way shown with dashed lines are recommended, but may be implemented only by mutual agreement of the City and property owner(s) with fair compensation to the owner(s). The property continues to be regulated by the underlying zoning (e.g., RN-C, RN-COR etc.).

ARCHITECTURAL STANDARDS

J	I	H	G	F	E	D	C	B	A
House	Duplex, Triplex & Quadplex	Bungalow Court	Rowhouse	Live/Work	Courtyard Housing	Hybrid Court	Stacked Dwelling	Liner	Commercial Block

BUILDING TYPES ALLOWED BY ZONE

	Building Type	Units/Acre Range [1]	Lot Width [3] (MIN–MAX)	Lot Depth (MIN)	Building Types and Stories Allowed by Zone [2] RN-C	RN-COR	NR	NS-E	NS-W
A.	Commercial Block	50 - 100	125'-350'	---	4-5	8 [2]	4	4	2.5
B.	Liner	30 - 70	170'-350'	100'	4-5	6 [2]	4	---	---
C.	Stacked Dwelling	50-100	125'-200'	130'	4-5	8	4	---	---
D.	Hybrid Court	40 - 50	170'-200'	130'	4-15	8	4	4	---
E.	Courtyard Housing	20 -35	140'-200'	130'	3	3	3	3	2.5
F.	Live/Work	15-18	25'-150'	110'	3	3	3	3	---
G.	Rowhouse	15-18	25'-150'	110'	3	3	3	3	2.5
H.	Bungalow Court	10-15	140'-180'	110'	---	---	3	2.5	2.5
I.	Duplex/Triplex/Quadplex	10-15	50'-100'	110'	---	---	---	2.5	2.5
J.	House	6-10	35'-60'	110'	---	---	2.5	2	2.5

--- = Not Allowed

[1] Dwellings (units) per acre per the typological limits of each building type and the range of dwellings that can be accommodated while maintaining the particular characteristics for the type as described in this code.

[2] See zone requirements for additional height information

[3] Measured along the front of the lot.

Working with Copy Editors

▶   How might a designer best work with code reviewers, town architects, and other copy editors?

When studio faculty review students' design work, they are acting as copy editors, attempting to improve projects without becoming coauthors. Similarly, design review boards, zoning officials, and others review projects for their compatibility with articulated public goals.

As project design practice becomes more national and international, designers are less likely to be expert advocates of localities. Thus, civil editors may feel compelled to develop regulations to steward the character of a place. Understanding design codes and design review as the work of editors rather than merely a set of administrative hurdles can aid give-and-take between project designers and stewards of the city.

The line between copy editor and coauthor can become fuzzy, and this may be one of the most conflict-ridden relationships between civil composition roles. Clarity about the goals and methods of the copy editors' role can help design authors work effectively with them.

Cartoons from *American City Magazine*, March 1923. The campaign to establish zoning in the United States argued that individual design actions were not adequately providing for the public welfare, and that zoning would prevent poor tenement design and protect home values.

Achieving systemwide collective goods frequently requires that individual projects conform to a set of practices. It is the copy editor's *primary* job to ensure reasonable compliance. Authors, of course, also are entrusted with these collective goods, but they are balancing those with a client's particular set of private goals. A client, to take an extreme example, may feel willing to risk not having a second fire exit from a third-floor office. However, to protect users, future owners, and firefighters, design of fire exits is reviewed by copy editors.

Many of the collective goods that copy editors seek to ensure are not so clear-cut. The public value of most setbacks, for example, is nebulous. Modernist architects may disagree with Santa Barbara's insistence on its variety of mission style. However, copy editors are not the people who select the collective goods, so arguing with them about the validity of a policy is ineffective. Venue editors, such as the city council, are typically the appropriate parties to petition to revise policy.

Balancing multiple goals and interpretation of particular cases, however, is within copy editors' scope. Asking for interpretations and clarifications early is a more effective practice than waiting to argue after a design is completed. Likewise, providing reasoning that supports an interpretation and respects the public goal is more compelling than trying to waive compliance.

It may be helpful to understand, and help copy editors follow, good practices for their role. In a defining case, U.S. Supreme Court Justice Brennan concluded that "any authority wishing to impose design review on individuals must demonstrate a community 'commitment'… and a 'comprehensive, coordinated effort' to raise design quality as a precondition of regulation."[3] In his article outlining best practices for design review, John Punter, professor of urban design, proposes four categories of principles:

1. ESTABLISHING A COMMUNITY VISION: The public must be involved in defining the collective goods that design review aims to achieve.

2. USING A BROAD ARRAY OF GOVERNMENTAL POWERS: The government should have a coordinated and comprehensive set of policies to achieve the stated collective goods. This effort should include not only regulation of private design but also use of government's capital outlays, commissioning practices, tax policy, or other powers.

3. DEVELOPING BROAD, SUBSTANTIVE, AND OPEN DESIGN GOALS AND PRINCIPLES: The program should include a full range of collective goods, such as accessibility and sustainability, and promote variety and innovation in the means of achieving the goals.

4. ESTABLISHING STRUCTURES FOR DUE PROCESS: Ensuring that design review is performed by people with appropriate skills in a transparent and effective process that includes a record of decisions and means for appeal.[4]

Civil designers who present their cases within these four principles both help their argument and may help improve the process of design review.

In addition to working for municipalities and other governments, copy editors work for developers, insurance companies, banks, associations, and nonprofits. The U.S. Green Building Council, for instance, trains people to verify LEED certification. The principles of review by a bank, developer, or nonprofit differ from governmental review but should clearly establish the scope, methods, flexibility, skills, and appeal process for copyediting.

In addition to understanding and working with the principles of copy editors, design authors should articulate and defend their responses to the unique conditions of their contexts. Otherwise, systemic uniformity will replace rich, layered, and meaningful diversity. The relationship between design authors and copy editors plays on the balance between order and variety.

▶▶ *Individual designers should understand the role and best practices of copy editors, seek to work collaboratively by respecting public goals and discussing issues early based on articulate reasoning, and advocate for meaningful variety and complexity.*

Field Testing

▶   How might design authors help design editors test
and refine proposals, plans, policies, and regulations?

Design editors propose and steward zoning codes and
regulations, built form types and patterns, tectonic systems,
venues for projects, and other design systems. Civil designers
of individual projects can help bring nuance and life to
these larger practices by articulating the benefits of specific
contexts and arguing for variety within order, testing proposed
systems for unintended consequences and opportunities,
and developing methods to study the internal and contextual
life cycle of a built project.

The U.S. Centers for Disease Control and Prevention's
mission to protect the nation's health depends on the
collaboration of individual doctors and organizations.
Similarly, editors of zoning, building codes, development
plans, and other systems need mechanisms to understand how
their work affects individual projects in different contexts, and
civil designers should actively seek to give feedback to editors
of these systems. Ideally this feedback should be articulate
descriptions of how the regulation or system could be altered to
continue to fulfill its aims while adapting to specific instances.
For example, the designer of a sidewalk coffee shop might
suggest that off-street parking requirements be reduced or
eliminated for defined "pedestrian-oriented" retail buildings
near transit.

Commissioning editors working as design columnists
and book authors can also benefit from constructive and
illustrative feedback from individual practitioners. Often this
occurs through questions after a lecture, panel discussions,
and letters. Some authors, such as Alexander, have established
nonprofit organizations to build a collaborative network
around their vision.[5]

Feedback to site developers, designers of larger
domains (e.g., neighborhood park designers briefing subdivision designers), and other venue editors is often bound up
in business relationships and legal obligations. However, both
sides can benefit if open and clear mechanisms for feedback,
dialogue, and adaptation can be established. This could
include postdesign debriefing, which can establish new tools
for future joint projects.

In a more proactive mode, designers could employ
their skills at creative interpretation of rules to beta test

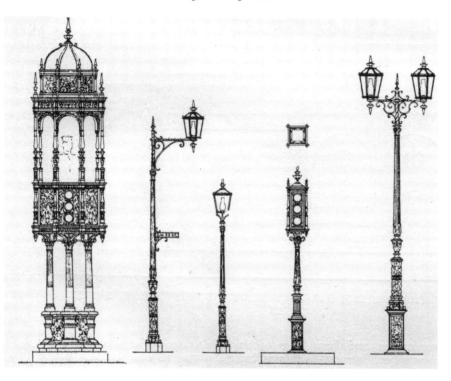

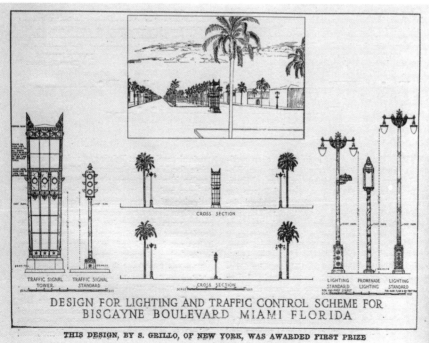

DESIGN FOR LIGHTING AND TRAFFIC CONTROL SCHEME FOR
BISCAYNE BOULEVARD MIAMI FLORIDA

THIS DESIGN, BY S. GRILLO, OF NEW YORK, WAS AWARDED FIRST PRIZE

proposed new policies, regulations, and plans, looking for loopholes and unanticipated consequences. Perhaps university design studios, professional organizations, or other groups of designers could conduct mock design trials by sketching projects that conform to but purposely stretch the proposed regulations.

Civil designers can also conduct detailed, long-term case studies of their projects to build a body of data about how design proposals play out. Perhaps a postoccupancy design phase should be created that includes testing and tuning components, ongoing measurement of environmental systems and user satisfaction, on-call design services for alterations and additions, decommissioning, and study of how the project acts in and affects its contexts over its lifespan. For instance, in what measurable ways did a community garden help revitalize a neighborhood? Did others follow precedents set by the project? Was the built form readily adaptable to new uses?

▶▶   *Work with design editors to test and refine their systemic propositions. Help articulate the benefits of the variety of contexts and individual conditions to which the proposed or adopted system should adapt.*

opposite
A traffic-control and streetlight design competition with a first-place winner by S. Grillo and a second-place winner by H. Roy Kelley, from *American City Magazine*, December 1926. Competitions are one method that design editors can use to promote and refine built species. In the 1920s, street lights and traffic signals were part of local urban composition, not a generic industrial design and engineering exercise.

Becoming an Editor

▶   Why might one become a design editor?

A parable is often used to explain the concept of public health
to medical students:

> Standing by the edge of a river, you see someone floating
> down the river drowning. You jump in and save him. Just as
> you get him to shore, you see another person drowning.
> You jump in and save her, and again you see another. You
> realize that you are faced with a dilemma—do you keep
> saving individual lives, or do you go upstream to find out
> who is throwing them in?

Moving from violinist to conductor, lawyer to judge, or
landscape project architect to urban forest manager is moving
upstream, from case-by-case to systemic practice.
    Why might one take on an editing role—conducting
design review, drafting codes, advocating new built-form types,
designing the urban form of infrastructure, or making urban
design schemes? In many ways, design authors already perform
some systemic tasks, such as developing a broad knowledge
of multiple contexts, designing for collective goods, and
coordinating the work of designers whose projects are within
theirs. Moving occasionally or permanently into an upstream
role is an extension of these tasks, and many people move
back and forth between roles. Fundamentally, it is a question

From an advertisement in *American
City Magazine*, May 1921. The advent
of outdoor electric lighting
transformed commercial streets in the
United States, creating a new
social-commercial nighttime milieu
often called "the great white way."

of interest and skill, similar to any choice of a calling. If you find yourself volunteering to rewrite zoning codes, sketching framework plans for the districts your individual projects inhabit, or researching ways to reconfigure a tectonic system, you have an interest in editing roles. However, it may be best to obtain a level of mastery as a designer first in order to know the details of a practice and empathize with designers. It is rare to have a great conductor who is not an accomplished musician on at least one instrument.

Developing the skills for an editing role is first a matter of becoming fluent in systems thinking.[6] A system is an interconnected set of elements that is coherently organized and produces its own patterns of behavior. Theater districts, appellation districts, and the concentration of high-tech companies in Silicon Valley are examples of systems. Systems thinking is the conceptual framework to see not just the trees, but the evolving forest. It is a discipline for seeing wholes, patterns of change, and interrelationships rather than things. Editors of civil systems should understand elements of systems theory, such as feedback loops (e.g., virtuous cycles); the critical importance of framing definitions of the boundary of a system (asking which contexts matter); and typical systemic problems, such as escalating rule-breaking.

Overview of Oxford, England. In addition to being a collection of college buildings, Oxford is the product of an evolving system of college founding and development. The courtyard pattern and many other aspects developed from a previous system: medieval cloisters.

Designing an individual built form, understanding and reframing its contexts, and contributing to collective goods, of course, all involve understanding larger systems. These skills provide a strong basis for taking on editing roles. Editing roles concentrate on rebalancing, managing, and developing multiple types of systems and thus require developing more advanced systems-thinking skills. Composing the infrastructure for a new transit village, for example, requires anticipating various ways this system could grow and mature through the actions of multiple designers and future regulators.

There are multiple paths for building editing skills. Cultivating an expansive and deep knowledge of a region's contextual history will help develop both systems thinking and a critical body of knowledge for regional editors. Participating in public forums, debates, and policy development will nurture collaborative management skills. The essential ability of systems editors is to follow systems across disciplinary boundaries. They can hone that skill by searching out an education in the principles, values, and language of civil design professions other than their own and by working with interfacing professions, such as environmental public health, land use, municipal, real estate, and environmental law.

Urban editors work for governments, nonprofits, academe, and developers (or sometimes they are developers). They are landscape architects, land-use lawyers, civil engineers, mayors and other public administrators, architects, and other civil designers. They have chosen, at least for a time, to go upstream and wrestle with systems of civil composition.

▶▶   *Develop your skills in systems thinking, participate in public forums, continue a broad study of contexts, develop a working understanding of related professions, and then consider where on the spectrum of roles your skills and interests fit best.*

Public Professionals

▶   What does it mean to be a professional?

> Conveniently, the English word *good* captures three distinct
> facets of work. Work may be good in the sense of being
> excellent in quality.... Such work may be good in the sense
> of being responsible—it regularly takes into account its
> implications for the wider community within which it is
> situated. And such work may be good in the sense of feeling
> good—it is engaging and meaningful, and provides
> sustenance even under challenging conditions.[7]

The term *profession* has an elaborate and often
contradictory semantic history, and definitions and
borders of individual professions evolve.[8] *The American
Heritage Dictionary*'s definition is "an occupation requiring
considerable training and specialized study."[9] However, other
definitions point to elements of professional infrastructure
that we should consider, such as a shared body of knowledge
or practices, licensure, continued study, commitment to high
standards of achievement and conduct, a shared sense among
members that the activity is, as Freidson writes, "a central
life-interest which provides its own rewards...something
that may on occasion be considered to be play," collegiality,
peer review and shared reflection, and a prime purpose of
rendering a public service.[10] Professions are often licensed,
and governments grant a monopoly to practice in return for

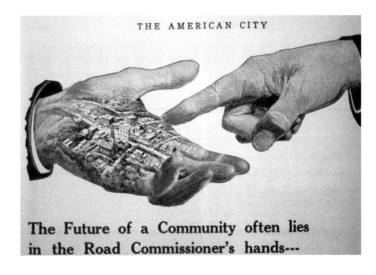

From an advertisement for asphalt in
American City Magazine, May 1922.
The creation of freeway bypasses
demonstrated the truth of the ad's
proposition that the decisions of a
road commissioner could profoundly
affect a community's future. The ad
also implies that even small decisions
can have long-term systemic
consequences, and thus professional
responsibility extends beyond the
immediate client and application.

THE AMERICAN CITY

**The Future of a Community often lies
in the Road Commissioner's hands---**

responsibility for a set of collective goods. Thus all professional civil designers have an editing or systemic charge. Being a professional, I propose, embodies all three aspects of "good work"—excellence, responsibility, and meaning.

Excellent urban composition, this book argues, includes actively understanding contexts and project roles, framing these contexts and developing designs to provide collective goods, and inspiring others to build on your work. Each individual project is an increment in the composition of a settlement.

Responsible civil design goes beyond the reasonable reach of regulations to consider what the cofounder of Architecture for Humanity, Cameron Sinclair, calls the ethical footprints of a project. This is the difference embodied by meeting the requirements for handicapped access versus striving for gracious universal design, grudgingly conforming to zoning versus participating in clearly articulating a community's public goals, or simply specifying materials versus shaping a tectonic market.

Moreover, responsible civil design rests on Jürgen Habermas's proposition that a "culture-debating society," in which participant-citizens create, partake of, and negotiate the meaning of cultural products, is preferable to a "culture-consuming society" in which we design either sets of total environments, such as Disneyland, or a variety of disconnected products, such as twentieth-century fast-food outlets and big-box retail stores. Perhaps one way to conceive of a professional field is the group of people whose work is to elaborate, argue about, and seek to achieve a set of systemic goals.

Professionals must therefore publicly propose their principles and, what is perhaps harder, be willing to modify them. How do your projects help create or modify the cultural landscapes in which they sit? What are the collective goods of your work?

▶▶   *Through education, dialogue, and their work, professionals share a body of knowledge and ways of seeing. They have a primary duty to promote a set of public goods, and to take responsibility for their "ethical footprints." Critically, professionals find joy in their work.*

Afterword

Civil designers can, and for the sake of our life on this urban planet must, collaborate. Our collective work is creating environmentally sound, socially resilient, and soul-enlivening settlements. We can collaborate by paying close attention to previous designs, their fit or misfit with their contexts, and their ability to support our civil goals. We can aim to knit together streets, districts, and larger cultural landscapes. We can make it productive for others to follow, work within, or elaborate our projects, and we can respect the range of roles from designers to editors.

Context-rich urban design that seeks to provide a set of collective goods in concert with works of past, present, and future designers is a more consequential and engaging activity than mere self-expression. Finding inspiration in multiple contexts, such as fictive landscapes, spatial practices, built species, and the means of construction; engaging in a built dialogue with other civil designers; seeking to provide collective goods; and searching for compelling meaning is the art of urban composition.

Kyrenia Harbor, Cyprus, composed over centuries by multiple designers serving in various roles.

Notes

Introduction

1. See Mark C. Childs, "Civic Concinnity," *Journal of Urban Design* 14, no. 2 (May 2009): 131–45.

2. See Robert D. Putnam, *Bowling Alone: The Collapse and Revival of American Community* (New York: Simon & Schuster, 2000); Charles Landry, *The Creative City: A Toolkit for Urban Innovators* (London: Earthscan, 2000).

3. Paul Goldberger, *Why Architecture Matters*, Why X Matters Series (New Haven, CT: Yale University Press, 2009), 219.

4. This discussion of concinnity draws from Childs, "Civic Concinnity," 131–45.

5. See Rob Keil, *Little Boxes: The Architecture of a Classic Midcentury Suburb* (Daly City, CA: Advenction Media, 2006); and Barbara M. Kelly, *Expanding the American Dream: Building and Rebuilding Levittown* (Albany: State University of New York Press, 1993) for discussions of the evolution of tract developments.

6. Jürgen Habermas, *The Structural Transformation of the Public Sphere: An Inquiry into a Category of Bourgeois Society*, Studies in Contemporary German Social Thought, trans. Thomas Burger (Cambridge, MA: MIT Press, 1989).

7. See Peter Hall, *Cities in Civilization* (New York: Pantheon Books, 1998); Landry, *The Creative City*; Richard Florida, *The Rise of the Creative Class: And How It's Transforming Work, Leisure, Community and Everyday Life* (New York: Basic Books, 2002); and Richard Florida, *Cities and the Creative Class* (New York: Routledge, 2005).

8. Hall, *Cities in Civilization*.

9. John D. Niles, *Homo Narrans: The Poetics and Anthropology of Oral Literature* (Philadelphia: University of Pennsylvania Press, 1999), 87.

10. See Kelly, *Expanding the American Dream*.

Contexts

1. William Cronon, *Nature's Metropolis: Chicago and the Great West* (New York: W. W. Norton, 1991).

2. Mathis Wackernagel and William Rees, *Our Ecological Footprint: Reducing Human Impact on the Earth*, The New Catalyst Bioregional Series 9 (Gabriola Island, BC: New Society, 1996).

3. Alexander Pope, "Epistle to Richard Boyle, Earl of Burlington," in *Alexander Pope: A Critical Edition of the Major Works*, ed. Pat Rogers (Oxford: Oxford University Press, 1993), 242.

4. H. W. S. Cleveland, *Landscape Architecture: As Applied to the Wants of the West* (Chicago: Jansen, McClurg, 1873).

5. Christian Norberg-Schulz, *Genius Loci: Towards a Phenomenology of Architecture* (London: Academy Editions, 1980). For other phenomenological approaches, see David Seamon, ed., *Dwelling, Seeing and Designing: Toward a Phenomenological Ecology* (Albany: State University of New York Press, 1993); Thomas Thiis-Evensen, *Archetypes in Architecture* (Oslo: Norwegian University Press, 1987).

6. Rachel Kaplan and Stephen Kaplan, *The Experience of Nature: A Psychological Perspective* (Cambridge: Cambridge University Press, 1989).

7. N. J. Habraken and Jonathan Teicher, eds., *Palladio's Children: Essays on Everyday Environment and the Architect* (New York: Taylor & Francis, 2005), 36.

8. Elinor Ostrom, *Governing the Commons: The Evolution of Institutions for Collective Action*, Political Economy of Institutions and Decisions (Cambridge: Cambridge University Press, 1990), 69–82.

9. See Ronald W. Haase, *Classic Cracker: Florida's Wood-Frame Vernacular Architecture* (Sarasota, FL: Pineapple Press, 1992).

10. T. S. Eliot, *The Sacred Wood* (London: Methuen, 1976), 48.

11. See Mark C. Childs, *Squares: A Public Place Design Guide for Urbanists* (Albuquerque: University of New Mexico Press, 2004).

12. Stewart Brand, *How Buildings Learn: What Happens after They're Built* (New York: Viking, 1994).

13. See Christopher B. Leinberger, *The Option of Urbanism: Investing in a New American Dream* (Washington, DC: Island Press, 2007).

14. Jane Jacobs, *The Death and Life of Great American Cities* (New York: Random House, 1961); Leinberger, *The Option of Urbanism*.

15. "History of the Municipal Art Society of New York," Municipal Art Society of New York, accessed June 26, 2011, http://mas.org/aboutmas/history.

16. "Perkins+Will Precautionary List," Perkins+Will, accessed June 26, 2011, http://transparency.perkinswill.com.

17. Pomegranate Center website, www.pomegranate.org; Architecture for Humanity website, www.architectureforhumanity.org.

18. Lyn H. Lofland, *The Public Realm: Exploring the City's Quintessential Social Territory*, Communication and Social Order (Hawthorne, NY: Aldine De Gruyter, 1998).

19. S. D. Joardan and J. W. Neill, "The Subtle Differences in Configurations of Small Public Spaces," *Landscape Architecture* 68, no. 11 (1978): 487–91.

20. Karsten Harries, *The Ethical Function of Architecture* (Cambridge, MA: MIT Press, 1997), 365.

21. William H. Whyte, *The Social Life of Small Urban Spaces* (Washington, DC: Conservation Foundation, 1980).

22. Louis I. Kahn, "Statement by Louis I. Kahn, Architect FAIA," Fleisher, accessed December 5, 2009, http://www.fleisher.org/about/kahn-room.php.

23. Jacobs, *The Death and Life of Great American Cities*, 2–3.

24. For other practices, see Oscar Newman, *Defensible Space: Crime Prevention through Urban Design* (New York: Macmillan, 1972); and Timothy D. Crowe, *Crime Prevention through Environmental Design*, 2nd ed. (Boston: Butterworth-Heinemann, 2000).

25. See Miguel Montiel, Tomás Atencio, and E. A. Mares, *Resolana: Emerging Chicano Dialogues on Community and Globalization* (Tucson: University of Arizona Press, 2009).

26. See Lawrence Durrell, *The Tree of Idleness, and Other Poems* (London: Faber and Faber, 1955).

27. This section is adapted from Mark C. Childs, "Storytelling and Urban Design," *Journal of Urbanism* 1, no. 2 (2008): 173–86.

28. See Ellen Dissanayake, *Homo Aestheticus: Where Art Comes from and Why* (Seattle: University of Washington Press, 1992); Jonathan Gottschall and David Sloan Wilson, *The Literary Animal: Evolution and the Nature of Narrative*, Rethinking Theory (Evanston, IL: Northwestern University Press, 2005); Niles, *Homo Narrans*.

29. See Carlo Rotella, "The Old Neighborhood," in *Story and Sustainability: Planning, Practice, and Possibility for American Cities*, ed. Barbara Eckstein and James A. Throgmorton (Cambridge, MA: MIT Press, 2003).

30. See Mindy Thompson Fullilove, *Root Shock: How Tearing Up City Neighborhoods Hurts America, and What We Can Do About It* (New York: Ballantine Books, 2004).

31. Gaston Bachelard, *The Poetics of Space*, trans. Maria Jolas (New York: Orion Press, 1964).

32. Terry Pratchett, *Witches Abroad* (New York: Harper Collins, 1991).

33. See Childs, "Storytelling and Urban Design."

34. Robert K. Barnhart, ed., *Chambers Dictionary of Etymology* (New York: Chambers Harrap Publishers, 1988), 1117.

35. Ibid., 241.

36. Herbert Gans, *Popular Culture and High Culture: An Analysis and Evaluation of Taste* (New York: Basic Books, 1974).

37. See Dennis Dutton, *The Art Instinct: Beauty, Pleasure, and Human Evolution* (New York: Bloomsbury Press, 2009); Kaplan and Kaplan, *The Experience of Nature*.

38. See Dissanayake, *Homo Aestheticus*.

Built Species

1. See J. B. Jackson, *The Necessity for Ruins* (Amherst: University of Massachusetts Press, 1980); and Mark C. Childs, *Parking Spaces: A Design, Implementation, and Use Manual for Architects, Planners, and Engineers* (New York: McGraw-Hill, 1999).

2. Childs, *Parking Spaces*.

3. See "Community Gardens," Trust for Public Land, accessed June 26, 2011, http://www.tpl.org/what-we-do/where-we-work/new-york/community-gardens.html.

4. Betsy Jarrett Stodota, ed., *Public Art Works: The Arizona Models* (Phoenix: Phoenix Arts Commission, 1992), 12.

5. Rud Okeson et al., City of Seattle in Superior Court of Washington for King County No. 77888-4.

6. Sam Bass Warner, *Streetcar Suburbs: The Process of Growth in Boston, 1870–1900* (Cambridge, MA: Harvard University Press, 1962).

7. Cleveland, *Landscape Architecture*.

8. Whyte, *The Social Life of Small Urban Spaces*.

9. Howard Davis, *The Culture of Building* (Oxford: Oxford University Press, 2000).

10. See Brand, *How Buildings Learn*.

11. See Open Building Strategic Studies website, www.obom.org.

Framing and Reframing

1. For use of the term in social science, see Ervin Goffman, *Frame Analysis: An Essay on the Organization of Experience* (Cambridge, MA: Harvard University Press, 1974).

2. Robin Dripps, "Groundwork," in *Site Matters: Design Concepts, Histories, and Strategies*, ed. Carol Burns and Andrea Kahn (New York: Routledge, 2005), 76.

3. Wendell Berry, *The Gift of Good Land: Further Essays Cultural and Agricultural* (San Francisco: North Point Press, 1981).

4. Ibid., 144.

5. The High Line design was led by James Corner Field Operations, with Diller Scofidio + Renfro. The initial section opened in 2009 and the second phase in 2011.

6. David Orr, "The Designer's Challenge," in *Encyclopedia of Earth*, ed. Cutler J. Cleveland (Washington, DC: Environmental Information Coalition, National Council for Science and the Environment). [First published in the *Encyclopedia of Earth*, May 16, 2007; last revised April 16, 2008; accessed December 7, 2009, http://www.eoearth.org/article/The_designer's_challenge_(speech_by_David_Orr)]

7. T. S. Eliot, *The Sacred Wood* (London: Methuen, 1976), 49–50.

8. Interactive Nolli Map website, nolli.uoregon.edu.

9. Daniel Dorling and David Fairbairn, *Mapping: Ways of Representing the World* (London.: Longman, 1997), 6.

10. Ibid.

11. See B. H. McCormick, T. A. DeFanti, and M. D. Brown, eds., *Visualization in Scientific Computing,*

Synopsis, IEEE Computer Graphics and Applications 7, 1987, 61-70.

12. Referring to mode of storytelling, see R. Gough, "Editorial: Mapping Theme Issue," *Performance Research* 6, no. 3 (2001); referring to art production, see D. Schultz, *The Conquest of Space: On the Prevalence of Maps in Contemporary Art* (Leeds: Henry Moore Institute, 2001).

13. Referring to James Corner, *Praxis*, no. 4 (2002); referring to Lawrence Halprin, *The RSVP Cycles* (New York: George Braziller, 1969); referring to Randolph Hester, "Sacred Spaces and Everyday Life: A Return to Manteo, North Carolina," in Seamon, *Dwelling, Seeing and Designing*.

14. Kevin Lynch, *The Image of the City* (Cambridge, MA: Technology Press, 1960); Hester, "Sacred Spaces and Everyday Life."

15. Dorling and Fairbairn, *Mapping*, 76.

16. See Merlin Coverley, *Psychogeography*, Pocket Essential Series (London: Harpenden Pocket Essentials, 2006).

17. As reported in Eckstein and Throgmorton, *Story and Sustainability*, 21.

18. "About the AIA | Programs and Initiatives: Regional/Urban Design Assistance Team (R/UDAY) Program," American Institute of Architects, accessed June 26, 2011, http://www.aia.org/about/initiatives/AIAS075372.

19. Tom Jones et al., *Good Neighbors: Affordable Family Housing* (New York: McGraw-Hill, 1995).

20. For example, see Orton Family Foundation website, www.orton.org.

21. Arlo Gutherie and Pete Seeger, "Preamble to *Quite Early Morning*," *Together in Concert* (Burbank, CA: Reprise Records, 1975).

22. See the Copyright Infringement Project at cip.law.ucla.edu for cases about U.S. musical copyright infringement.

23. Paul Spencer Byard, *The Architecture of Additions: Design and Regulation* (New York: W. W. Norton, 1998).

24. William Hubbard, *Complicity and Conviction: Steps Toward an Architecture of Convention* (Cambridge, MA: MIT Press, 1980).

25. Edward Bacon, *Design of Cities* (New York: Viking, 1974), 109.

26. See Byard, *The Architecture of Additions*, 32-36.

27. For a philosophical-poetic analysis, see Martin Heidegger, *Poetry, Language, Thought*, trans. and intro by Albert Hofstadter (New York: Perennial Library, 1971).

28. Habraken and Teicher, *Palladio's Children*, 70-71.

29. Ibid., 2.

30. See Childs, *Parking Spaces*.

31. See David Nye, *Electrifying America: Social Meanings of a New Technology* (Cambridge, MA: MIT Press, 1990); and William Mitchell, *City of Bits: Space, Place, and the Infobahn* (Cambridge, MA: MIT Press, 1995).

32. See Childs, *Parking Spaces*.

33. Thomas A. Markus, *Buildings and Power: Freedom and Control in the Origin of Modern Building Types* (London: Routledge, 1993).

Infectious Design

1. As quoted by Donella H. Meadows, *Thinking in Systems: A Primer* (White River Junction, VT: Chelsea Green Publishing, 2008), 12.

2. Bacon, *Design of Cities*, 109.

3. Kathy Edwards and Esmé Howard, "Monument Avenue: The Architecture of Consensus in the New South, 1890-1930," in *Shaping Communities: Perspectives in Vernacular Architecture VI*, ed. Carter L. Hudgins and Elizabeth Collins Cromley (Knoxville: University of Tennessee Press, 1997).

4. S. Russell Forbes, *The Aqueducts, Fountains and Springs of Ancient Rome* (Rome: Via Della Croce, 1899), 19.

5. See Christopher Alexander, *The Nature of Order: An Essay on the Art of Building and the Nature of the Universe* (Berkeley, CA: Center for Environmental Structure, 2002).

6. This section on virtuous cycles is based on Childs, "Storytelling and Urban Design," 173-86.

7. See Kingston Heath, "False-Front Architecture on Montana's Urban Frontier," in *Images of an American Land: Vernacular Architecture in the Western United States*, ed. Thomas Carter (Albuquerque: University of New Mexico Press, 1997).

8. Diane Favro, "The Street Triumphant," in *Streets: Critical Perspectives on Public Space*, ed. Zeynep Celik, Diane G. Favro, and Richard Ingersoll (Berkeley: University of California Press, 1994).

9. Hall, *Cities in Civilization*.

10. See Nye, *Electrifying America*; Warner, *Streetcar Suburbs*.

11. Christopher Alexander et al., *A New Theory of Urban Design* (Oxford: Oxford University Press, 1987), 66.

12. For more on teamwork, see J. Richard Hackman, *Leading Teams: Setting the Stage for Great Performances* (Boston: Harvard Business Press, 2002); Glenn Parker, *Team Players and Teamwork*, rev. ed. (New York: Jossey-Bass, 2008); Michael Schrage, *No More Teams! Mastering the Dynamics of Creative Collaboration* (New York: Doubleday, 1995).

13. Goldberger, *Why Architecture Matters*, 215.

14. Jacobs, *The Death and Life of Great American Cities*.

15. Ann Jarmusch, "Italian Renaissance," *San Diego Union Tribune*, February 14, 1999.

16. Eliot Freidson, *Professionalism Reborn: Theory, Prophecy, and Policy* (Chicago: University of Chicago Press, 1994), 176.

17. See L. J. Hanifan, "The Rural School Community Center," *Annals of the American Academy of Political and Social Science* 67 (1916): 130–38; Pierre Bourdieu, *Distinction: A Social Critique of the Judgement of Taste*, trans. Richard Nice (Cambridge, MA: Harvard University Press, 1984); Putnam, *Bowling Alone*.

18. See Putnam, *Bowling Alone*.

19. "EyeStop," MIT, accessed June 26, 2011, http://senseable.mit.edu/eyestop.

20. S. Nicholson, "How Not to Cheat Children: The Theory of Loose Parts," *Landscape Architecture* 62 (1971): 30–35.

Design Editors

1. The definitions of roles presented here is adapted from Mark C. Childs, "A Spectrum of Urban Design Roles," *Journal of Urban Design* 15, no. 1 (2010): 1–19.

2. Habraken and Teicher, *Palladio's Children*.

3. William J. Brennan Jr., "Dissent," *Members of the City Council of the City of Los Angeles v Taxpayers for Vincent*, 466 U.S. 789, 1984.

4. John Punter, "Developing Urban Design as Public Policy: Best Practice Principles for Design Review and Development Management," *Journal of Urban Design* 12, no. 2 (June 2007): 167–202.

5. See Building Living Neighborhoods website, www.livingneighborhoods.com.

6. See Meadows, *Thinking in Systems*.

7. Howard Gardner, *Five Minds for the Future* (Boston: Harvard Business Press, 2007), 127–28.

8. See Eliot Freidson, *Professional Powers: A Study of the Institutionalization of Formal Knowledge* (Chicago: University of Chicago Press, 1986); Freidson, *Professionalism Reborn*; and Thomas Bender, *Intellect and Public Life: Essays on the Social History of Academic Intellectuals in the United States* (Baltimore: Johns Hopkins University Press, 1993).

9. *American Heritage Dictionary of the English Language*, 3rd ed. (Boston: Houghton Mifflin, 1992), 1446.

10. Freidson, *Professionalism Reborn*, 200; see also Freidson, *Professional Powers*.

Image Credits